Y2K and the American Dream

A Practical Guide for Personal Millennium Readiness

Y2K and the American Dream

A Practical Guide for Personal Millennium Readiness

by
Mike Gaffney

toExcel
San Jose New York Lincoln Shanghai

Y2K and the American Dream
A practical Guide for Personal Millennium Readiness

Published by toExcel

For information address:
toExcel
165 West 95th Street, Suite B-N
New York, NY 10025
www.toExcel.com

ISBN: 1-58348-286-5

LCCN: 99-62424

Printed in the United States of America

Contents

Introduction

One of the most talked about topics in the news today is that of the coming millennium; that is when 1999 turns into 2000. People are just now starting to hear stories in the popular press about the so-called "Y2K" bug. Y2K is an abbreviation for "Year 2000" and it represents the fact that much of what we take for granted in the world today may have a hidden flaw which will suddenly render many of our automated staples of life useless. Over the last twenty years, computers have become an increasingly vital part of our everyday existence and suddenly within the next eighteen months; a threat to the efficient operation of these computers will strike.

Many news reports and books, that are becoming available, focus upon the effects of Y2K upon the corporate world and talks about computers and programs being "Y2K compliant". Be aware that the term "Y2K compliant" has no legal meaning or basis. In the coming year in major high profile Y2K related failure litigation cases, the courts will ask "compliant to what?" and "compared to what standard?" If the business world is still struggling with definitions and meanings, then imagine the status of the average citizen trying to comprehend it all.

Because of this confusion toward the approaching millennium period, this book focuses on the personal aspects of Y2K and how the failure of computers based in government and corporations all over the world can come to affect our lives. Despite what the title suggests, it will be of great interest to the general population of all nations who are interested in knowing how to properly prepare for the coming millennium and how to avoid becoming a Y2K victim.

Statistics reported in the USA Today in February 1999 stated that fully 68% of people polled expressed concern that the Y2K related problem would affect them personally and professionally. This book is written to help those growing number of people prepare for the effects of Y2K so that they can minimize the risk of serious impact by the millennium passage and the secondary business failures that will result from random and widespread supply-chain failures directly related to it. The text should be used to help the ordinary citizen prepare for the coming date change and the possible havoc that it will cause in our society, and even in our personal lives. The book is organized into chapters that will allow anyone, regardless of computer literacy, to properly prepare for this important event so that our lives will suffer the least amount of disruption.

It should be stressed that neither panic nor complacency is the correct response for the millennium period. There will be enough panic by the unprepared and that, by itself, will cause much of the havoc and damage that could be unleashed on our country, and many nations of the world as January 1, 2000 approaches and finally arrives.

What is outlined in this practical, common sense book is the result of exhaustive research and interviews and years of consulting in the information systems world. It is organized into an easy to follow set of steps that can be utilized to reduce the personal exposure to personal, financial, and societal risk. Think of it as an investment in keeping what you have worked so hard to attain. The Y2K and its associated fallout are sure to be a period that could wreak havoc on the unprepared.

The reader must realize that it may be impossible to eliminate 100% of the risk of personal and financial harm, and inconvenience associated with Y2K related fallout. What you can do by following the recommendations in this book is to reduce the risk of exposure to these factors to a point where you are prepared. It will help you build a plan for temporary survival if the worst of the forecasts are realized. It will also help you to build a plan for financial stability during a financially unstable period.

In the book, you will find a number of checklists in many of the chapters and in the appendix for you to review as you go through the book. In order to be truly effective, you should follow the recommendations that apply to your personal situation. Feel free to make whatever changes or additions you want to these checklists and risk assessment charts. The chapters are flow in a logical manner building the case of preparedness and financial preparation. Preparation over the coming months should be a priority for each of us. Some of the areas covered in the checklists may surprise you. Areas such as infrastructure and emergency services are items many people might not have considered as threatened by the Y2K. Why should we be worried about traffic lights not working, you might ask? The answer, you will find out, is not as obvious as you might think and has not yet captured the imagination of the press, but nonetheless is possible. In reality, if the computers that control our traffic signals in our cities are struck by the Y2K bug, there could be traffic jams and chaos that could suddenly affect our ability to get to work or to pick up our kids from school and daycare centers.

As a final thought, your position after completing this book is not to be one of the panic–stricken masses. You don't want to become part of the problem and be tempted to pull money out of the stock market. There will be enough economic damage from people doing this out of ignorance and fear. This book is not advocating the purchase of a so-called "Y2K Survival Kit" that is already starting to hit the market. You do, however, want to take whatever precautions to protect yourself, your loved-ones, and your belongings. If you can, you can even take advantage of the situation because you are prepared. You will have a plan and that will be a large part of the solution. You will be very glad that you did!

The Y2K Problem
—What does it mean to you?

Many of us have heard stories on TV and in the paper about how the "Y2K bug" could affect the businesses and governments in the world around us. No one has ventured forward to describe how it will affect each of us as an individual, because no one knows for sure what will happen and how the problem will manifest itself. If they did, there might be more excitement and effort toward overall readiness for the millennium period. So far, many of the reports have talked about how various computer systems might crash if the Y2K bug is not fixed. They also have talked about how many countries in the world have done little to address the problem, yet.

Why should we, as citizens of the greatest country the world has ever known, be concerned? The answer lies in the fact that we now live in a global economy and that what happens elsewhere can affect us fairly quickly. We were forced to open our eyes to this fact during the summer of 1998 with the Asian financial crisis. At first it seemed that their problems would not affect us, but sure enough, and much faster than people expected, the problems soon spread to other areas of the globe, including the United States. It finally took a personal turn when our IRA and Mutual Fund statements in October 1998 reflected as much as 15–20% loss of our wealth disappearing in a period of one financial quarter! We now started to realize that despite the fact that we were imminently content with our economy and our lives, we could be affected quickly by factors that were completely outside of our control.

The implications of the Y2K are different though. This is a problem of hidden dimensions and proportions. We don't know exactly what is going to happen and how it is going to affect us. It is mainly a computer and technology oriented event, but we now live in a world that is surrounded and operated by computers and technology. Any computer or electronic device that has a clock or a calendar function built into it is susceptible and must be evaluated for its failure affect on our businesses, our employers, our banks, and our own lives. You will soon find out that not all devices with clocks are going to fail, and in fact, most won't. But you need to know how to tell which ones will in order to properly protect yourself.

There are different levels of risk during time phases approaching during and after the actual millennium transition time of 12:00 midnight, December 31, 1999. The susceptibility of the technology that surrounds us cannot be isolated or simplified to a specific minute of time. The problem will manifest itself in a much more subtle and insidious manner. You will soon find out in this book that the *millennium period* is not a single day event but is rather a series of events spread out over an eighteen-month period. In order to properly prepare for the effects and consequences, it must be understood what things are likely to happen in what portions of the *millennium period*.

How could this Y2K problem have happened and why is it just recently that people are starting to worry about fixing it? The answer lies in the way that computer programmers think and work. In the 1970s and 1980s, programmers were writing programs driven to run as fast as possible, and use as little room as possible on computers that were extremely expensive. Mainframe computers cost millions of dollars and had power little more than what many people have in their office computers today. As a consequence, programmers were concentrating on compressing their program's use of disk and memory space in order to meet departmental budget constraints. They found that a database or data storage file with millions of records took much less space if the date was stored as a six digit text character such as "031584" then to store it as a date such as "03/15/1984". They would then use another set of program code lines to turn the "031584" into a number and then perform sorting, printing and arithmetic functions on the number and then reconvert it back to the date format to store it in the database. Typically, a program would place the year first, followed by the month and then the day (i.e.: 840315, 840316, 840317) so that sorting would be correct. When the program was done with its stated function, the code would turn the number representing the date back into a non-number text character and restore it back in the database in its original form. The programs started to get more and more elaborate as programmers started to write routines that calculated weekdays and weekends in any given year and to determine leap year, etc. This convention spread as more and more programmers were taught in school and from their peers that this was an acceptable practice.

Few seemed to be concerned (with the notable exception of Apple Computer whose systems have always been *Y2K ready*) until the early 1990s. Insurance companies performing statistical and actuarial table analysis started to discover errors in their actuarial table calculations that spanned enough years to cross the millennium date of January 1, 2000. By then, it was too late. Programmers had been writing programs this way for nearly 30 years. The problem had been spread around the globe in computer programs and computer chip driven devices everywhere. Many of the devices we use in our homes such as VCRs, TVs, coffee makers, and time stamp cameras were consequently written by programmers who used the same techniques to program the computer chips that are integral to the electronics of the device.

Why can't we just go out and fix the problem? Many companies are now becoming very much aware of the cost, scope, and magnitude of the program and are addressing budgets and resources to fix the problems. In many cases, they have started far too late to test and fix every possible place that an error could occur. The problem is that there are literally tens of billions of lines of program code that have been written. For instance, a typical purchasing system used by a Fortune 500 corporation could contain as many as three million lines of program code. Think of the problem of getting modern day programmers to go back through all of those lines of program code, many of which were written 15 to 20 years ago, looking for these errors and then instituting a correction. Then think of the monumental task of testing all of the programs and applications to make sure that the fixes are correct and have not inadvertently broken something else. Since no two programmers write code in exactly the same style, there is not a precise way to write a program routine to fix the errors automatically. How do we know that the programmers that are fixing today's problem code are using programming style that will not cause another problem to occur? Once a change is made to a program, it must be thoroughly tested to make sure that the fix in the date code did not break some other aspect of the program that the programmer did not realize or intend to be affected. The result of all this testing is a multibillion dollar time and resource problem in the US federal government alone. Imagine the costs of this repair and testing effort across all of the corporations in the US and other international companies. The numbers are purely staggering.

What about commercial and private industry and the effort they need to expend to find the Y2K problem in their systems? Who pays for the effort here? In the end it will be us, the customers. But in the meantime, what has happened is that companies and governments have put off the expenditure of the funds until the last minute. Many experts and consultants who are monitoring the progress of the Y2K testing and repair program now report that for many organizations, it is too late. They have simply waited too long to get the amount of experienced programmers necessary to fix the problem in time. Many companies are doing the best they can with the resources they have, but the probability of missing critical date programs and routines without thorough testing is great.

You can start to see that the problem has a far-reaching implication and it is inevitable that the results could have some kind of impact on you and your lifestyle. One question that needs to be addressed is what kind of effect will it have and will it be a temporary inconvenience or will it be a serious problem that could cause great harm in terms of safety or financial stability to each of us personally.

The answer is that we just don't know how bad the problem will be and we do not know how long the problem could last once it does manifest itself on our lives. It is because of this that we are starting to hear stories of people who range in response from taking radical steps toward preparation to taking a "who cares" attitude. How you will personally use the information in this book and from other reliable sources depends on your disposition to invest time in preparation to avoid the unknown risks of an approaching event with unknown consequences.

In the press, it was recently reported that Israel is facing a major Y2K related problem that is different from anything discussed in this book, so far. It appears that certain religious groups believe the coming millennium to be the "Second Coming of Christ". They have embarked on a process of giving away all of their earthly belongings and purchasing a one-way ticket to Jerusalem so they are present for this holy event believing that they will be saved, as a result. My point is not to pass judgement on their belief or comment on its credibility, but what happens to these people if their belief does not come to pass?

There also have been reports that certain militant centric survivalist groups in America believe that the millennium will represent the collapse of the American federal government. As a result of this belief, they are stockpiling weapons, food and supplies. Apparently, they believe that in the chaos and confusion of the "Y2K bug" computer and technology failures of government and industry, masses of people will try to rush them, desperate for supplies and food in an effort to purely survive.

Both of these examples represent what many "mainstream" citizens of most modern nations might consider radical or extreme, yet they are a reality of what some believe are the necessary steps to prepare for the coming event. While we have these "extreme" responses on one hand, we have a whole other set of examples of people who are willing to risk it all and are viewing the event as a huge party. There are reports of people throwing lavish events on the top floors of high-rise buildings, almost tempting fate. Which of these response extremes will your response are most like? That becomes your own private decision. The coming chapters will address the steps that you need to consider regardless of where you fall between the two ends of the spectrum in regards to this event.

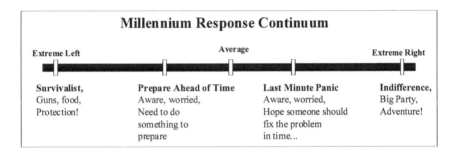

Let us take a quick look at how the problem might affect us personally. A seemingly innocent example was mentioned in the introduction regarding traffic lights and how computers control their timing in large grids on our city streets. What if there is a problem in the computer programs that control these traffic signal grids and the ability of the programs to reason with the fact that the year no longer starts with "19" and now starts with "20"? Suddenly we may have entire city street grids with blinking red lights causing massive traffic congestion. This has a domino affect because now people can't get to work and trucks can't deliver supplies to grocery stores, etc.

What if you have an airline reservation or an electronic ticket for a trip for business to meet with your largest client and you get to the airport and the airline system has failed because of a Y2K bug and the airport is standing still? Once again we see that in simple ways, this problem can turn from somebody else's problem into our own in a hurry.

The question becomes how can we prepare to deal with something which we have little control over? That is what this book will address for you. It will help you to identify the potential risks, and help you to build a plan for your personal life that will avoid the mass confusion and havoc that could occur for at least the first several weeks after the date change in January 2000. In the example of the traffic, the solution could be that you arrange with your employer to work from home with your computer the first week or two of the year 2000, thus avoiding the worst of the problems, should they occur. In the case of the airlines, you could plan ahead and make sure you have a paper ticket issued instead of an electronic ticket, or you could postpone planning your trip until the third week of January. Just taking steps like these could save you a considerable amount of time and trouble. Remember that the biggest effect of the millennium will be economic fallout from supply-chain failures and resulting business failures. These effects may take months to occur!

As you follow along in this book, you will notice that each chapter will address a host of similar situations that you could encounter in the year 2000 while the authorities and the programmers try to sort out the systems that are causing the problems. These items are all important, and you may think of several others that are not mentioned. By all means, add them to the checklist so that as the weeks draw near to the date switch, you will be ready to keep your life in order.

You, like many people in our world today, are probably a very busy person and may be apt to think that you haven't got the time to devote to something that may, or may not, happen. There are some areas addressed by this book that should really deserve your attention, regardless if you have enough time to worry about traffic lights.

One such area is that of personal finance. Most of us have taken the steps to begin to plan for our financial future. We may have opened an IRA or even enrolled in a 401K at our place of employment. We have taken the steps to invest in the stock or bond market or purchased shares in some mutual funds as a way to save money for our future. What would you do if you received a statement from your Mutual Fund in January 2000 that stated the account balance was a fraction of what it was the quarter before? Normally we would call customer service and have them research the problem, look at last months statement on their computer or their report, and correct the error. But, what if the same error that happened to you happened to that institution's other million shareholders simultaneously as a result of a Y2K related error in some of their programs that calculate interest? This suddenly would catch your attention and become worth your time taking some precautions to safeguard your fortune.

There are a number of steps that you can take to avoid this type of problem. Many of the specific steps are covered in future chapters. We will, however, say that preparation and knowledge will be the key to success in these and related matters. The Securities Exchange Commission (SEC) has issued a ruling that makes it mandatory for financial service firms, brokerages, banks, and fund operators to prepare and submit a "Y2K" readiness statement. In addition, most publicly traded companies are now required to report on their Y2K readiness efforts in their SEC annual filings and their annual reports. Just because a company says they are working on the problem does not mean that you are completely safe from harm, but it is comforting to know that the US Government is compelling action to minimize the effects of the millennium passage. If you are a citizen of another country, you need to investigate what your government is doing to ensure the safety of your financial markets.

It should also be comforting to know that most American companies have a keen awareness of the risks of this problem and are addressing it to the best of their resources. Large companies in other nations are also looking at Y2K readiness but it is questionable whether many smaller commercial companies in foreign countries have taken Y2K seriously in time to avoid business interruptions. The problem with many companies and businesses becomes one of what we call "supply-chain". Supply-chains will be described completely in the next chapter, but for now, consider that anyone or anything that provides a necessary ingredient to another entity is part of a "supply-chain" or supplier to that next entity. When the supply-chain is broken or interrupted, there is a measurable effect on that receiving entity and any entity upstream in that supply-chain. From this simple explanation you can see that a simple failure or interruption at any point in a supply-chain causes a cumulative effect.

A Company that manufactures automobiles may depend on thousands of small businesses to provide parts and sub-components. If anyone of these suppliers is unable to fulfill their commitments because of a Y2K failure, then there is a domino affect on the rest of the supply-chain. So, just because the auto manufacturer certifies that they are *Y2K ready* doesn't mean that a problem won't occur. This one example of one automobile manufacturer could be multiplied by thousands of businesses up and down the supply-chain of the global economy.

The US Government Accounting Office released one estimate stating that the cost of Y2K related litigation and damage costs could reach $1 trillion dollars. This amount of damage when applied to our economy and the economy of the world is sure to have some impact on each and every one of us. No one should be able to completely escape the effects of this monumental event. It becomes our personal responsibility to look around us and look at the companies, government agencies, institutions, and service providers that directly and indirectly affect our lives and make whatever arrangements that make sense to protect ourselves from a temporary disruption in that service or product. If we don't, we risk being a statistic or worse, a victim of Y2K.

Once again, the reader could be tempted to draw the conclusion that they are helpless to address problems for which they have no control. Let me assure you, there are things that you can do to minimize the chance that you will be adversely affected. I stress the concepts of preparation and investigation and will continually refer to them throughout the book as a way to determine your risks and then find ways to mitigate them. Through the use of the checklists contained in the subsequent chapters of the book, you can build a plan that contains all of the alternatives and contingencies that will make the difference in the Y2K related fallout on your life, and possibly the people around you.

I was recently talking to a company in the general-aviation business. One of the managers told me that their biggest worry regarding Y2K is whether they will be able to get fuel for the airplanes in the event of a "supply-chain" failure affecting the fuel distributor at the airport. My recommendation to this manager was to establish an alternative fuel agreement with another company, at another close airport that received their fuel from a completely different supplier. The agreement should be a contingency contract that only applies in the event that it is needed. This agreement should be drawn up well in advance of the actual millennium passage so that it is put in place with a minimum of strings attached. This is an example of how this contingency process can work in business as well as in our own personal lives.

Let us define what we mean by investigation and preparation. Then let us look at how they can be used in the time remaining between when you read this and December 31, 1999 to ensure a successful passage into the year 2000 and into the months that follow.

Investigation is the process that you will use to look at the risk of, and effects of, disruption by the providers of services and goods that directly and indirectly affect your life. There are a number of methods that you can use to investigate your personal "supply-chain". We mentioned earlier that organizations such as the automobile manufacturer and the aircraft rental company have a "supply-chain" and they are subject to business disruption if one of the links or suppliers in their supply-chain has a Y2K related failure. Just in the way that these companies are interested in investigating their suppliers, so must we, as citizens, be interested in the same thing. If by way of investigation, we find out that your financial institution or broker might not be ready for the Y2K, or does not have the courtesy to take your inquiry seriously, then you have an option to move your business to one that makes you feel more comfortable. Perhaps the proper response and preparation for the millennium is to set up a second bank for our personal finances. We can split our finances between the two unrelated banks to make sure that if there are problems at one, we can still go to the other. This is called diversification and is a very important aspect of the preparation process.

There are a number of ways that you can investigate your suppliers. One common method is by telephone. Many organizations have set up special customer service agents who address Y2K related inquiries. In fact, they may just send you a form letter saying that they are working on the problem, but at least that is something. One bank that I deal with has issued a pamphlet explaining the Y2K problem and their status in dealing with the problem. The bank does a credible job of describing their plan to identify potential problems, correct the problems, and then retest the systems to make sure that all of the problems are properly addressed. The fact that they have taken this step indicates to me that they are actively working on the problem and want me as a customer to be aware that I should not be worried about them as my supplier. Just recently, I noticed that this bank now posts a "Y2K Readiness" message on their ATM screens. They are doing the best job they can to let their customers feel comfortable with them as a supplier.

Another common way to investigate is through the use of the Internet. Since statistics show that many of the people who will read this book also have a computer with Internet access, I believe that it is important to address this as a viable method of investigation. There are two ways that you can use the Internet to investigate. One is that you can visit the website for the companies that you are interested in learning about. Many websites will have a special link to a Y2K update page that may contain information similar to a newsletter. As you look at the information on the page, look to see if there is a date of the last update. If the information appears old or hasn't been updated in a while, then it may be time to call the company and check on the progress. If the website doesn't have a specific section regarding Y2K, then use their website search engine, if one exists. The important thing for you to know about your supplier is that they are aware of the Y2K related problem, they are working on a resolution, and they are sensitive to your rights and interests as their customer to know how their readiness will affect you personally. If your supplier does not respond with information that is to your satisfaction, then maybe you should consider diversification with that supplier similar to the way many companies are building supplier contingencies in their supply-chains.

The second element of the investigation/preparation process is preparation. You basically have two options regarding your response to the coming millennium. You can sit back and do little or nothing and hope that everyone else works out the problems, or you can be actively involved to prepare yourself for the inevitable inconveniences that will arise. I advocate the latter option. I think that you will find that with a little bit of work, you too can be ready. In order to know how to prepare, you need to know what your risks are. Once you identify your risks, through investigation, then you can proceed to the preparation stage.

Suffice it to say that I am not advocating panic for this event, but rather I am advocating preparation and the use of a systematic evaluation of risks and appropriate responses. Only you can be the judge of what is an acceptable risk to yourself personally. I will provide you some examples of risk levels of things that might occur and some responses that you can take, if you so choose. You must evaluate through your own investigation whether these or other items not mentioned are important enough, or pertinent enough, to warrant preparation.

For instance, if you identify by investigation that there is a risk of ATM machines not working immediately after the January 1, 2000 date change, then you can prepare by getting some extra cash in the months before the critical date. I would not advise waiting until the last week of December 1999 to get the extra cash because you will be standing in long lines with everyone else.

If you identify that there might be a risk of not getting your payroll check through electronic bank transfer, then you may want to prepare by switching back to a manual check for the first several months of the year 2000.

If you believe that there is a risk that you may not have a consistent supply of electricity due to the electric company's Y2K related failure of their transmission grid, then you can prepare by having candles and flashlights available. Once again, preparation will be the key. Lots of people will be buying candles in December 1999 as the media heightens its coverage of potential problems in the last weeks of December. Preparation means that you thought of it far enough in advance that you got the items on sale and without waiting in line.

You may be starting to think that this Y2K problem could be a major inconvenience to you. You may be right. Personally, I am optimistic that things won't be as bad as some reports are saying it might be. However, my research shows that there are a lot of areas that are weak links and I have decided that it makes far more sense to be ready then to be sorry. Hopefully, you the readers will take advantage of this important and timely information so you won't be standing in line at the ATM on December 31st,

1999 or worse yet on January 1st, in the event that the worse of the predictions comes to pass. By being knowledgeable of the risks and asking lots of questions of our suppliers of goods and services, we can cause others to think about the effort that they need to exert in order to mitigate their business risks that might inadvertently affect us. No one in business wants to suffer a loss of customers or business through a fault that may, or may not, be unavoidable. The sooner that businesses come to grasp with the effort that will be required to test, fix, and redeploy their systems and machinery, the better off our chances of minimizing the impact of the Y2K bug will be.

Personal Supply-chains

So far we have explored the Y2K related problem and looked at some ways that it can affect our businesses, our families, and us. In order to understand the event and the problematic fallout that will be associated with it, we must look at the chain of events that can possibly occur that will eventually having some impact or inconvenience on us.

One way to analyze the systematic series of events to determine the risk of service interruption is what is called "supply-chain" analysis. Supply-chain refers to the entire sequence of information, inputs, labor, or raw materials necessary to produce and deliver a product or service. Most organizations have identifiable supply-chains. Organizations that produce a product receive raw materials or assembled sub-components from suppliers and after a series of internal processing steps turn those materials into finished product that is required by the end user or another supply-chain entity.

In a globally connected society, we can guess what happens when a supply-chain for a necessary product or service is interrupted. Take for instance the example of what happened to General Motors in 1998 when they had a strike at one of their parts plants. Without the parts flowing from that parts plant to its assembly plants, within a week production capacity at all of their plants across North America came to a halt. Once the labor dispute was resolved, it took almost a week to replenish the supply-chain with the necessary materials to recall the rest of the workers and resume pre-dispute levels of production. I would be willing to bet that there were other issues internally that took even longer to work out before things were back to normal. The result of this month-plus long work stoppage resulted in a multi-billion dollar quarterly loss for the giant corporation.

Why would companies keep such a limited amount of inventory on hand leaving themselves vulnerable to supply-chain disruptions? It turns out that many production plants minimize the stock they keep on hand for financial reasons. This stems back to the 1970s when the Japanese made popular the practice of "just-in-time" inventory control. "Just-in-time" works very well when you have a well-disciplined manufacturing process with an efficient logistics control system to provide the necessary parts and supplies. It tends to minimize parts inventory and all of the financial and warehouse assets required for managing it. But it has its drawbacks, as GM found out with the work stoppage in 1998.

The problem occurs when anything happens to upset the balance of this supply-chain process. It really can be anything in the supply-chain that causes a big enough disruption to deplete available contingency reserves. It could be labor, raw material, components, sub-components, utilities, or computer inputs. One of the functions of corporate management of a company is to set standard reserve levels for critical supply-chain materials to preclude a work stoppage under most circumstances. This has become increasingly important in recent years as companies have attempted to manage their supply-chains more closely using sophisticated supply-chain management software. One of the responses that I see occurring in preparation for Y2K is a tightening of controls over supply-chain. Companies are increasing their inventories of critical supply-chain components and identifying alternative suppliers that will be called upon in the event of a supply-chain interruption.

What does this have to do with the citizen? The answer lies within several aspects of supply-chain management. It therefore becomes a critical factor in determining how Y2K will affect each and every one of us. First of all, each of us has a supply-chain for all of our goods and services that we receive. We also are part of a supply-chain for other aspects of our everyday lives, such as providing labor or intellectual property to our employers. Mainly we are the recipients of the supply-chain for those goods and services we end up buying. We may find that if a supply-chain is broken or disrupted as it flows to us, then we not be able to fulfill our role as a component of the supply-chain that we take part in. A good example of this is that a disruption in oil and gasoline delivery to our local area caused by a failure in control computers at several major refineries may directly affect our ability to get to our jobs. We saw this occur in our own country in the late 70s with the Arab Oil embargo. Do you remember sitting in long lines waiting for our respective turn to get gasoline at the few service station outlets that has not yet run out of fuel? Do you remember how tempers flared as people were frustrated that they could not fill their tanks and could not get to work? This was an extreme example of a supply-chain disruption that affected many of us directly and therefore affected upstream supply-chains that we were apart of.

There are lots of examples of supply-chain that are around us everywhere, highlighted by the gasoline shortage story above. We can look at the utilities that flow into our house as one very direct example. There are a whole chain of events and suppliers that have to work in order for electricity, gas, water, cable-service, and phone service to operate correctly in our homes. What is the effect if any one critical aspect of any of these utility services breaks down? We can have a service interruption. We have come to largely take for granted the availability of these services that few of us ever stop to consider the possibility of service disruption. Could this kind of failure happen as a result of the Y2K event? That becomes a topic that will be explored in upcoming chapters of this book. The point that must considered is that if such a service inter- ruption of critical utilities or other services does happen, how widespread will the problem be and how long will it last? What will it take to fix the problem, especially if there are similar problems occurring simultaneously around the globe?

In the example of utility service disruption, there is a two-sided problem. The same utility suppliers that supply us personally also service everything else in our towns and cities. Do you remember the case of the 12-hour power outage in San Francisco last year? It was caused by a power grid problem that overloaded a number of critical power substations that supplied power across the entire San Francisco municipal area. The entire city and the surrounding communities came to a screeching halt. The BART subway system and the famous trolleys would not move. Traffic was snarled because no traffic-control devices were functioning. People waited outside of their office build- ings and apartment buildings. Security guards would not let them into the buildings without elevators and fire protection systems operational. This was an extremely frus- trating experience for many, many people who otherwise took for granted the continual supply of power to their city.

With the power problem, it is not as easy as simple on and off when it comes to Y2K. Many in the power industry are warning of power "brownouts". If you look at how the power industry works and how it regulates the power that flows to our homes and businesses, you see that there are very distinct patterns of power output which are computer matched to meet power consumption demand. This consumption demand fluctuates with the time of day, the day of the week, and the month of the year. These demand/supply management functions are provided by very sophisticated time and date management software that attempts to manage the power flow to the grid to ensure uniform voltage.

The problem with Y2K and power supply is two-fold. First of all, many companies are shutting down their factories and buildings in hopes that they will avoid the problems associated with the transition to year 2000 at midnight on December 31. This causes an unknown demand factor on the power grid that may cause power fluctuations. This will result in power surges in some places and inadequate power in others. The problem is multiplied on Monday morning, January 3, when all these companies begin to power back up all the equipment that has been off-line for that weekend. Suddenly there is a huge demand for power that can overload many powergrid substations resulting in unstable power supply. Experts in the power industry have cautioned that they do not know exactly what the consequences of these fluctuations will be. The problem in both of these cases is not limited just to the convenience aspects of the power supply fluctuating. The main problem is that many types of sensitive equipment cannot withstand such power fluctuations and there could be secondary equipment and computer failures associated with the power fluctuations themselves, even if they were "*Y2K ready*". This is what we call a "secondary Y2K failure". Many Y2K secondary failures will be confused with primary failures and it will take months to sort out the differences. The net result is that we should expect problems in the power-related supply-chain and everything that depends upon it.

Examples of such equipment in a household would include TVs, computers, printers, stereo and surround sound control units, satellite dish control units, fax machines, and answer machines. If you want to properly prepare for the Y2K, you may want to consider leaving your voltage sensitive equipment turned off, or make sure that the equipment is connected to surge protectors and universal power supplies. These devices will ensure that your equipment does not suffer as a result of a power related supply-chain failure.

Could these kinds of failures happen as a result of the Y2K event? This becomes another interesting question that we will explore in coming chapters of this book. Again we must consider that if it does happen, how widespread will the problem be and how long will it last? If we want to minimize our risk exposure to the Y2K bug, than we need to include such steps in our millennium plan that will anticipate power fluctuations caused by supply-chain failures or variances.

Another example of supply-chain related problems that could affect us is employment. Yes, that's right, employment! Many of us work in industries that involve manufacturing and assembly related jobs. Earlier, we gave an example of what happens when a supply-chain related failure hits a manufacturing plant like the General Motors manufacturing plants example discussed previously. This is a perfect example and one that we want to explore further.

We already suggested that one of the Y2K related preparations of large companies be the performance of a detailed analysis of their critical supply-chains to look for any signs of supply-chain weakness. An example of such a weakness might be a sole-source supplier of a critical component to a manufacturing or assembly process. The procurement managers for the manufacturing company would determine that the supplier was a mission-critical supply-chain component. They will begin, if they haven't already, to ask some very pointed questions about that company's preparations for Y2K. They will also ask some very tough questions about any of that supplier's supply-chain providers and their vulnerability to Y2K related failures. The procurement managers will also begin to look at alternative sources for that critical part or component in the event that there is a Y2K or secondary failure in that supplier's ability to deliver that good or service. With the identification of other sources for that good or service, the receiving company will feel that they have adequately covered their weak link in their supply-chain. The procurement departments of companies all over the country, and for that matter the world, are performing this very task. This is good news for the larger companies, but it also poses a threat to the smaller and more vulnerable members of the supply-chain.

What happens on the days immediately following January 1, 2000 when, through no fault of their own, one of these smaller providers suffers a direct or secondary Y2K or supply-chain related failure? As soon as the larger company detects the problem by virtue of the failure to deliver the critical supply or service, the larger company switches suppliers to the alternative supplier cutting off the business to that smaller supplier. One way that you can look at this is from the viewpoint of survival of the fittest. What happens when this is multiplied to a global basis, and from a macroeconomic viewpoint, this supply-chain thrashing occurs simultaneously around the world? This will have a devastating effect on the global economy as well as the local economies of the people affected by the suppliers that are possibly put out of business.

This is a perfect example of why the supply-chain is the single largest threat resulting from the Y2K. Many people believe that the Y2K failure is something that will happen on January 1. I believe that the majority of failures and damage associated with Y2K will not be felt for weeks or even months after the Y2K passage event itself. This makes the Y2K a larger threat than many people believe. The implications concerning Y2K related economic disaster are far larger than the direct effects of the failures of computers to deal with the time and date by itself. This is one of the reasons why many people in the world, including most Americans, are only just beginning to acknowledge that they might be affected by the Y2K. They have not begun to appreciate the role of their supply-chains and their roles in larger supply-chains. These facts are some of the major premises for this book, and hopefully you are beginning to appreciate the gravity of the supply-chain issue on Y2K related preparations.

As you continue on through this text, you must recognize that your personal supply-chain and the effects of service or product disruptions is little different than the example of how the corporate procurement managers are treating their suppliers. You must take a hard look at who is in your supply-chain and evaluate the consequences of temporary or extended disruption in the delivery of that product or service to your family, your business, and you. When you identify that you have a sole-source supplier, you need to consider whether you can line up an alternative supplier of that good or service. You may or may not be able to accomplish this, such as with the case of your electric utility. But in other cases, you may be able to make such a diversification such as with the case of your bank, your credit card, your debit card, and your gasoline supplier. The important thing, as you will soon discover is the importance of starting this preparation process early. You will soon see that there are a number of very specific "*millennium periods*". By knowing these periods and what is likely to occur in each, you have the best chances of properly preparing for the inevitable inconveniences or supply-chain failures or threats that are likely to occur in that period. The following sections of this text devote specific planning actions that can be taken in each of these periods.

As was stated earlier, the basis and foundation for the composition and research of this book is macroeconomics; the study of the interaction of large scale economies and the reaction of the economic entities that make them up. supply-chains of both businesses and personal enterprises are the entities that make up the whole global economic climate. Each of us is, in some way, part of some supply-chain, whether supplying-labor to our employers or capital as a consumer. It becomes clear to see that any major and geographically dispersed disruption such as Y2K is bound to trickle into our lives. It is because of this that we must have discipline if we want to avoid being a victim of the greatest threat to our economic viability this century. Indeed, the Y2K related threat to supply-chains will become a substantial threat to the American Dream.

Corporate and Government Preparations for Y2K

As you look around you, the press and the media are starting to report more and more about corporate and government preparations for the millennium. One reaction I hear from many people is that they are waiting to form their opinions about whether they should worry about their own preparations for Y2K. (Remember the chart on Millennium Response Continuum?) These people's rationale is based upon their belief that the government and corporations are spending billions of dollars preparing for Y2K and this should solve the problem for them.

This book is dedicated to helping the citizen and the small business operators prepare for the Y2K. In order to help you understand the full extent of threat and to see where the fallout will occur; we must explore the larger scale preparations on the part of our governments and corporations. We can learn from their lessons in relation to our own needs and preparations. What have the large organizations accomplished with all of billions of dollars they have spent on Y2K preparation? Has all this effort really reduced the threat of catastrophic computer failure for these organizations and does this help to protect us? This chapter is going to explore the government and corporate preparations for Y2K and help you to conclude your own opinion about whether their preparation should allay your own personal concerns. You may, in fact, end up being more concerned.

The fact is that the US government and US based corporations have literally spent tens, if not hundreds of billions of dollars since 1996 on Y2K related testing and system changes. There are a number or areas that these organizations have focused their resources and attention on.

If you have been watching statistics from a number of sources relative to government Y2K related preparations, you will agree that the numbers are truly staggering. If only the original designers of these computer systems had foreseen the ramifications of their early time and date algorithms, think of the possibilities that this tax money good have offered to society! The problem that we must contend with is that Y2K is so much more deeply imbedded into our nation's computer infrastructure than many believed. Many of these systems are twenty and nearly thirty years old. Not only are the computer languages that were used to write these programs obsolete, but many of the programmers who knew these languages have long since retired or moved on to more modern computer architectures and programming languages. This means that in order to find people who could use the special search tools to wade through billions of lines of computer code, you had to look for people with skills that had not been used for many years. Many organizations have sought out the original programmers and paid them extremely high rewards to bring them back as consultants. Many were even brought back from retirement!

What did all of this accomplish and did it work? The answer is a qualified yes. The systems of the largest US government agencies state agencies and corporations have been drastically improved. However, it is impossible for these organizations to guarantee that there will be no problems with their systems, even after spending all of this capital to fix and test these systems.

Let us look at the anatomy of a typical, complex computer system currently operating in private, government, and commercial organizations all over the US and around the world. A typical computer system is made up of hundreds, to sometimes thousands, of user screens, reports, and programs that interact with each other running on the computer's operating system. Each of these screens, reports and programs are written using one of dozens of possible computer languages and may contain thousands of lines of computer code each. It is not unusual for a single corporate or governmental mainframe computer application to have several million lines of computer code. Note that this application is one of hundreds of such applications running at the same time on the same, or networked, computers. That equates to tens, if not hundreds, of millions of lines of computer code that may be running at any given organization or agency at any one time. Multiply this by all of the governmental agencies and commercial companies and you get tens, if not hundreds, of billions of lines of computer programming code dispersed on computers located all over the world. You are now beginning to see the sheer magnitude of the Y2K related problem. In order to truly assure a successful and error-free transition to the year

2000, every one of these programs must be scanned and corrected of susceptible time and date related program code that contains the Y2K error.

Additionally, another aspect of the Y2K problem is that the databases that contain date information stored in the abbreviated two-digit form must be also corrected. Remember, years ago the pioneer programmers searching for space efficient programs set up databases to contain only two digits for the representation of the year. Do they now "expand" the database fields to include the four-digit date or do they change the program to assume "19" or "20" in front of a date?

Sometimes this data cannot be corrected without manual intervention. Take for instance the case of the Swiss man reported in January 1999 in USA Today, aged 104, who received notice that he should report to the grade school registrar to register for elementary school. The date in the database had his birthday ending in "94". There was no automated way for the computer to know whether he was born in 1894 or 1994! How could you correct this data in the database to assure that the newly written or Y2K corrected program could interpret the birthday correctly? The unfortunate truth is that there is no sure way to correct this type of problem without manually validating each and every record or somehow cross referencing some type of social registration number such as the Social Security Number to assume the century based upon valid number ranges. This example is a seemingly harmless example of what can turn into a nightmare for millions of people after January 1, 2000.

Not let us look at the testing effort that must be employed to find a so-called Y2K bug that may be hidden anywhere, in any one, of these lines of code. The Y2K related software problem offers the greatest challenge to testing and validation of software programs to see if they will malfunction when the time and date read various times in the year 2000. They must be tested to make sure they will work at the stroke of midnight on January 1. This is referred to as the "millennium transition time" and offers the largest threat to many systems that will be running at that time. Systems and applications must also be tested for random dates in 2000 and 2001 as well as on February 29, 2000, a leap year.

The problem with many of the computer applications today is that they contain literally hundreds of functions and reports that may have date calculations or date algorithms. Every time a program is changed or altered, presumably to correct a Y2K related software code defect, someone needs to test the software to make sure that the problem has been fixed, or that the fix hasn't caused other unforeseen problems. A software-testing engineer will tell you that every conceivable menu option must be exhaustively tried and examined to ensure that the problem has been adequately remedied. This becomes a daunting task for someone and typically, a major information systems shop will employ dozens of people whose job it is to test their software for errors of any kind. The problem with the Y2K bug is that the testers must simulate the date change to January 1, 2000 as well as verify proper operation on February 29, 2000 to ensure that the program will properly deal with leap year.

The process of testing to this level of detail requires more time than most shops have manpower or budget, so another more automated method had to be devised to accomplish the task. There are computer software companies that offer special applications to scan computer programs for the Y2K related problem. Companies such as *Compuware Corporation* offer industrial strength programs for testing mainframe and client-server (network distributed) computer applications. Companies such as *Norton Utilities* offer special programs to search your home and office computer looking for Y2K offensive code as well as Y2K viruses. These solutions have proven to be very attractive to larger organizations who have employed software like Compuware's *QA Center* and *Hyperstation* to automate and track the progress of a specific set of test data and test results through a wide range of possibilities of user keystrokes and data input conditions.

The process of completing the Y2K bug fix consists of a number of steps in order to ensure that the job is done correctly and completely. The steps are *application inventory, prioritization, scanning, repair or replace, unit testing, integration testing, stress and load testing, and acceptance testing.*

Let us look at each of these steps individually so we can comprehend how difficult it is for companies and government agencies to guarantee a "Y2K error free" system. This is an important step for each of us to properly assess our risk exposure and determine to what level we want to depend upon others for our Y2K related preparations.

The first step in Y2K systems certification is *application inventory*. Believe it or not, many organizations did not have a complete and exhaustive listing of all of their computer applications, let alone know which ones might contain computer code susceptible to the Y2K error. In the days of mainframe only applications, application inventory was easier to track but now, with the proliferation of distributed architecture computer applications, it has become difficult for the information systems department to keep up to date and manage all of the possible computer applications in their portfolio. This is especially true for ones that may have been created by an end-user and distributed across departmental server computers without the specific controls required by centralized data processing.

Once all the computer applications are inventoried, they must be *prioritized* in terms of importance to the business. Someone must go through each application and look at criteria such as frequency of use, mission criticality, integration or importance to other applications that share data, the importance of the application to management or key end users, etc. During the course of this evaluation, it becomes pretty clear that some applications have a top priority to the business and some may not matter to the business at all. Some applications that may have seemed important but turned out not to be and visa versa. The important thing is that companies need a way to determine that given limited time and resources for Y2K preparation, some applications must be worked on before others in order to minimize Y2K related impact if they run out of time.

Once the applications have been prioritized, they are now ready to be *scanned* for Y2K errors. The scanning process can be done using one of several methods. They may be manually scanned by doing searches across lists of programs for known keywords relating to time and date functions or they can be scanned by using automated search tools. Either way, there is a possibility that some Y2K bugs may slip past the scan function and it must somehow be caught later in the testing functions before the program gets put back into production. Many companies have decided to outsource both the *scanning* and the *remediation* functions to outside vendors such as *Compuware, Cap Gemini, and IBM*. These vendor companies and others have set up so-called "software factories" to scan and correct large quantities of computer programs sent to them by client companies. Typically, a company would load hundred of programs onto disks or tapes and send this off to their chosen vendor. Upon receipt, the vendor who would complete the task and return the corrected tapes back to the company for final testing and certification. Although this may be the most consistent way to search for and correct the highest percentage of pure program errors, this approach will lose its effectiveness if the company does not perform a thorough test of all application code upon return from the vendor. The vendor typically does not have a method of testing the interaction of the programs together with databases and other programs and applications. This leaves open the possibility that something has been overlooked. If implemented with the right level of quality assurance controls in place, the companies who can afford to use this approach and employ a specific "quality control" methodology to thoroughly test all aspects of program functionality stand the highest probability of assuring "Y2K readiness" to their customers.

The next step in a thorough Y2K test process is *remediation or replacement.* This step occurs when it is determined that a program or application has Y2K susceptibility and requires some kind of intervention in order to avoid a Y2K related problem. The company typically will analyze whether it makes sense to fix an application or replace it with a new application or packaged software such as *Peoplesoft* or *SAP*. Two years ago it made sense to consider replacement of a software application such as payroll, procurement, or order entry with a packaged solution, but as the clock counts down to Y2K, it is no longer feasible to assume that such a undertaking could be success- fully completed in time. Industry statistics suggest that the cost of implementing an integrated Enterprise Requirements Planning (ERP) package solution can cost up to five times the cost of the software acquisition itself. Much of this cost is spent in the area of training and consultant costs and the costs associated with conversion of legacy (original) data and databases to work under the new environment. Because of this huge expense in terms of elapsed time and labor, companies who have not already under- taken such a package implementation effort by late 1998 probably will wait until after 1st quarter 2000 before resuming plans to implement a packaged software solution.

The same problem holds true for application development plans. Many companies that were very active building and deploying point and enterprise-wide applications have all but halted plans until after the millennium passes. They have instead diverted funds toward Y2K related testing, completion of packaged application implementation, and completion of any custom development projects that were already underway. Many of these companies are reporting that they will "freeze" their application production environments during 2nd or 3rd quarter of 1999. This means that no new applications, databases, or programs will be allowed onto the corporate computers and networks after the "freeze date". They use the rationale that they want no risk of a new appli- cation or program somehow corrupting an otherwise "Y2K sterile" computer envi- ronment. Few can dispute the wisdom of this decision, although this is already having repercussions in the software application development tools marketplace as procure- ment of these products is coming to a halt during 1999.

Many companies have decided to fix or repair the existing programming code prior to the "production freeze" date instead of "outsourcing" the function to an outside soft- ware-factory. In this case, it must assign the various programs and database pieces of the application to a programming team that will look for the Y2K related problems using a manual or automated process. Line by line, the program must be examined and rewritten until the Y2K errors are found and fixed. Once the programmer certifies that the program or programs he is working on are *"Y2K ready"*, then the program is returned to the Y2K program office for testing. In order to ensure that all programs are bug-free, they must undergo several different testing procedures.

The first of the testing procedures is *unit testing*. Unit testing is when an individual program is tested with simulated test data or inputs to ensure that it performs its intended function. It is important that the test procedure be established prior to programming work to establish a testing baseline to compare results against. This is important to make sure that the program is not unintentionally damaged during the Y2K repair.

Most programs have input and output parameters that can be used as "handles" to test with. For instance, a program whose function is to perform a calculation of sales tax has two input parameters called *"subtotal"* and *"taxrate"* and two output parameters called *"salestax"* and *"grandtotal"*. In unit testing, you test that particular program by passing into the program a value such as "450.00" and a tax rate input value of "0.05", it should return back test result output values of 22.5 and 472.5. If it does, than the program has passed the unit test and can be moved on to the next phase of testing. If it fails, then it must be passed back to the programmer for rework.

Typically, a unit test procedure must be more comprehensive than passing a single test. A good test plan would include a range of input values that would test for various conditions including error conditions so that there is no possibility that the program would crash later or inadvertently cause an error in another program. In our example of tax calculation, other test data input parameters might include "0", "free", and "-450.00" to make sure that all bases have been covered.

The sales tax example is simple compared to what needs to be done for Y2K testing. In a Y2K test, the operating system date in the test system needs to be changed to 12/31/1999, then 1/1/2000 and then 2/28/2000 during each of several test runs to make sure that the program runs properly in all three millennium date conditions. Imagine being the test engineer responsible for testing every single application program in an entire organization.

Some organizations leave unit testing to the programmer and others have separate testing groups responsible for unit testing. Regardless of how an organization handles its internal test process, each program must be individually tested before the programs can be reassembled into an application for integration testing.

Many organizations feel so rushed by the whole Y2K related problem that they are only getting as far as unit testing and are putting their applications back online. This can be a dangerous assumption to make because there is no assurance that the fixes made to any individual program or procedure are compatible or consistent with other programs that must inter-operate with it to form a working application.

This is the role of *integration testing*. Integration testing is the process where all the individual programs and procedures are reassembled and operated in a simulated computer production environment to make sure that the entire application works properly and that it meets or exceeds all user expectations and requirements. In this type of testing, the system date is presumably independently and progressively reset to the three critical millennium dates and sample test data or users operate the system to make sure that it functions correctly. Any discrepancies or variances from acceptable results are documented and may result in the application or individual programs being sent back for additional work with the programmers and or testers. In a tightly controlled testing environment, the entire test process would have to be restarted from *unit testing* forward. This makes sure that no additional errors are reintroduced during the program repair process.

The next major step in the testing process is *stress and load testing*. This is when the software application is put through a simulation representing a realistic number of users or transactions occurring simultaneously. Too many times a system is put into production too soon only to find that its architecture cannot withstand the load of production demand. Y2K testing is no exception. Any organization that implements system changes to critical business applications without completing a thorough load test is asking for trouble in terms of strain on the business, loss of credibility with the users, or both.

The final step in testing systems applications prior to full production implementation is *acceptance testing*. This is the final step and represents where a controlled sample of the users test the system and provide their final acceptance of the application inclusive of all changes, repairs, and additions.

Looking at the preceding chain of steps necessary to constitute comprehensive testing, the reader may get the feeling that it is likely that few organizations will have the time or resources to test everyone of their hundreds of business applications to this level of detail. What level of confidence of "Y2K readiness" is enough to prevent a supply-chain failure? What level of "Y2K Readiness" is achieved with each progressive step of testing omitted due to time or budget constraints? Many organizations are struggling with these very questions, not because they want to, but because they simply do not have the resources to completely do the job right.

Certain industries have less tolerance than others for margins of error. The Securities and Exchange Commission (SEC) has mandated financial institution and bank compliance with "Y2K Readiness" by June 99 or those organizations could face stiff penalties or sanctions. The Nuclear Regulatory Commission has mandated that nuclear powerplants certify 100.0% readiness by July 1999 or face shutdown. This particular issue is very critical because it takes nearly 4 months to shut down a nuclear reactor due to cooling and residual radiation concerns. Reports from that industry report considerable debate about how to ascertain 100% "Y2K readiness" and confusion about what Y2K readiness conditions will dictate that the reactors to shut down in July 1999.

There are several other problems with conducting "fool-proof" testing of applications in a corporate or government environment in the interest of certifying Y2K readiness.

First, many organizations do not have the computer operational capacity to assign to a testing environment. Distributed networks are nearly impossible to simulate for testing conditions and few organizations have more than test regions specified on a small portion of the available processing space on organizational mainframe computers.

Second, few network administrators would have the time or the bandwidth to provide all the work necessary to reset all of the system operating system clocks to simulate the Y2K condition without executive mandate. This might be due to the complexity of time synchronization across multiple network servers and their respective operating system clock and calendar functions. This pushback will not stop the test, only delay its execution.

Third, there is an inherent risk in prematurely initiating a primary or secondary software failure associated with changing time and date to a point in the future. Not only can this cause a premature system failure, if there is a Y2K related problem, but it can also cause other software problems to occur. One such example is software license management. When date parameters are exceeded, certain software functions may be triggered shutting down vendor software perceived to be "out of contract" due to expired licenses.

Fourth, and perhaps most important is the input and impact of remote system interface with computer systems outside of the primary control or jurisdiction of the testing organization. Today, many computer systems are integrated with, or interface to, remote computers for the purpose of sharing data and information. This growing trend toward E-commerce and Electronic Data Interchange (EDI) has exploded since the late 1980s. Some pioneer companies such as Wal-Mart made it a prerequisite for suppliers to be able to communicate order, shipment, and billing information electronically to cut the cost of backoffice administration of their businesses. This trend quickly spread across the US and into other countries at an accelerated pace during the 1990s. It is nearly impossible to coordinate all of the possible data sharing sites to simultaneously simulate Y2K date changes as the testing companies' test. Therefore, the integration test must be conducted independent of remote data feeds or using static or simulated data. This does not guarantee that the application being tested will survive a condition where Y2K corrupt data is sent from a remote data-sharing computer on January 1, 2000 and beyond.

There are many examples of this data sharing that will become particularly troublesome during the millennium period. The Internal Revenue Service receives data inputs and has remote data interfaces to many different organization's systems. Examples of other organizations the IRS might interface with include the fifty State Revenue departments, companies payroll departments to share withholding data, H&R Block for electronic filing, the Social Security Administration, the Labor Department, and others. Any one of these external organizations could inadvertently send Y2K corrupt data to the host computer causing a Y2K related problem or failure.

Another example of extensive data sharing is in the law enforcement community. Local police departments receive and send data to and from state centralized criminal record registries as well as from the FBI and the NCIC nationwide crime database. What is the effect of one organization sending Y2K corrupt data to another? It is possible that this facilitates a chain reaction of system failures because the central registry passes the corrupt data on to other sharing entities?

Looking at the various US government agencies and many corporations' Y2K readiness statistics leaves little room for blind optimism. Even after spending billions of dollars to exhaustively test their internal systems, there could be no guarantee that their computers running Y2K sterile programs and data won't be corrupted by receiving Y2K corrupt data from an external data or computer source that has a Y2K related error. There really is no way to tell whether this will happen until January 1, 2000 and beyond. This becomes one of the single most uncertain aspects of the millennium that few experts will even speculate upon.

We saw in the preceding chapter what it takes to execute a thorough testing procedure in accordance with a testing methodology. You can probably see that in order to complete a test of this level of depth, the time and resource requirements are enormous. This is true for small organizations as well as for large ones. The trouble is, we are running out of time available to conduct this kind of thorough testing before the millennium date of January 1, 2000 arrives.

I was in the US Post Office the other day and noticed the Y2K countdown clock rapidly going through its paces as part of an advertisement for a millennium stamp collection. The counter said 299 days, 12 hours, 9 minutes, and 14 seconds, and was counting down the seconds rapidly. This is the type of pressure that many of the corporate and government agencies Y2K project managers feel. The available time is speeding toward the showdown. There are far too many things to do and systems to test in the time remaining. There has been a mixing of priorities and budget availability over the past several years since the Y2K related threat was identified. Now that the deadline looms near, all of the budget in the world might not be able to reduce the risk to an acceptable level.

Although I would have preferred to keep the topic simple and non-technical, I fear that I may have failed some of you. This chapter was included as a necessary part of explaining how corporations and government agencies are dealing with the threat so that you, the layperson, can understand the rhetoric and the flip-flop reports you are hearing in the press and other media. Stay with me though, because now you have been through the entire process of learning how the Y2K problem was created and what it takes to keep it from seriously affecting our families, our companies, our government, and ourselves. It is a technical problem but it will cause problems all around us of various sizes and descriptions.

So what does all this mean to the average citizen of the average industrialized nation? It means that we must digest all of the information about Y2K, its threats, its promise, and the rhetoric and statistics of readiness with a cautious eye. We must accept the possibility that just because someone declares that they are *"Y2K ready"* does not mean that they are immune from harm. The fact is that they may have done everything they can to minimize risk, but there is still exposure and we must determine if there is anything that we can do to diversify our exposure as a result of that risk to minimize the possibility of personal harm or inconvenience. In the end, it all comes down to fate. Those who minimize their exposure have the least likely probability of ill effect, and this is what each of us should strive for.

Millennium Time Periods

So far, we have explored the Y2K related problem and looked at what government and corporate organizations are doing to prepare for it. In the coming chapters we will start to look at the personal effects of Y2K and a structure of how to prepare ourselves for the coming event.

It is important to recognize that there are different periods for the millennium that logically organize the anticipated risks and reactions into predictable categories. Through all of my research and interviews, I have identified four distinct periods that I call "millennium time periods". It is around these four periods that the rest of this book is based. The following timeline chart summarizes the four periods:

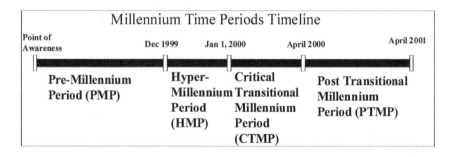

These categories have been established in order to properly categorize and assess the risks of the millennium to the ones we care about and ourselves and. We also needed to break down the millennium transgression into time periods that we can use throughout this book to facilitate an effective checklist process for the readers.

The first time period is called the *Pre-Millennium Period* (*PMP*). This is the phase that we are in right now. It lasts from the point of initial awareness until approximately the end of November 1999. The point of initial awareness is different for different people. I have found that many people have been cognizant of the Y2K related problem since 1996 and have been busy in their organizations trying to build testing plans that would be used to get their organization ready for the millennium. Others point of awareness is only recent. Most organizations have been looking at Y2K as a threat at least since 1998. What is your point of awareness?

The next period is the *Hyper-Millennium Period* (*HMP*). This phase essentially begins in December 1999 and lasts right up until Midnight, December 31, 1999. It will be marked by rapid sweeping panic and surging short-term interest rates as people attempt to stock up on cash and supplies based upon media reports and hype that will begin decidedly toward the end of the holiday shopping season.

The next phase is the *Critical Transition Millennium Period* (*CTMP*). This phase will last from 12:01am January 1, 2000 until March 31, 2000. It will be marked by the actual time and date change to the year 2000 and all of the failures and side effects that goes along with it.

The final phase will be the *Post-Transition Millennium Period* (*PTMP*). This period spans from the end of 1st quarter 2000 until the end of 1st quarter 2001. This will be the period of financial and global market instability caused by business failures and Y2K related litigation. It will also mark the recovery period from the millennium passage as markets begin to recover during the period. There will be an emergence of new companies, new products, and new ideas. It will be a kind of renaissance.

These time periods are very important because they establish the criticality of preparedness of certain aspects of our lives depending upon the risks of Y2K failure of societal, business, and infrastructure elements that we depend upon. The most critical failure period for electronic devices, electrical powers systems and things that run on the electrical power systems is the *CTMP*. We are at low risk of a Y2K related failure and its effects for electrical devices during most of 1999 because the date error has not been introduced into the programs that control them. This is the time that we should be doing our investigations, diversification, evaluations, testing and preparations. This is also the best time to be reevaluating our financial portfolios and considering reallocation of our investment ratios in order to diversify our holdings. We are at a much higher risk for banking or a billing error during the *CTMP*, but that risk continues on through

June of that year as programs that run on quarterly billing cycles are subject to undiscovered failures and effects. The risk of financial errors and tax system problems will continue to run high through June of 2001 because many of these systems are run much later in the calendar or fiscal year and may still encounter undiscovered Y2K stricken data or programs causing failures. The later chapters in this book will detail the specific steps that need to be taken in each of these millennium phases.

One of the things that you may notice that is different with the approach of this book and the other sources of Y2K related information that you see is that the *millennium periods* spread the period of risk out over a predetermined, extended timeframe. As we have stated, the millennium and its effects are not concentrated on a single day or days. It is really a whole series of loosely related consequences that occur over a period of time. As you will se in the coming chapters, the single largest problem that will result from the millennium change will not be the computer failures themselves. The single most devastating fallout of the millennium will be the effect on the economy of the US and the rest of the world caused by business failures resulting from disruptions in the international supply-chain.

These supply-chain failures will only start to be felt during the *Critical Transition Millennium Period*. Mainly, they will be felt in the *Post-Transition Millennium Period* that begins in April 2000 and continues for 12 months after that.

Few people that I talk to in my lectures and consulting engagements have considered the possibility of the extended millennium periods, let alone are prepared for that kind of extended economic impact that I believe that is not only possible, but probable.

Most of the media reports that you hear and the articles that you read seem to concentrate the millennium and the Y2K related problem into something that occurs on January 1 and then seems to fade away with the fireworks that will usher in the New Year. Unfortunately, my research suggests that the effects will actually linger on for a considerable period of time. The effects will be concentrated in seven main groups called "millennium impact categories".

In order to organize our understanding of what can possibly occur in each *millennium period* and to best prepare ourselves for the inevitable inconveniences that will occur, we have identified these specific categories that are most likely the highest areas of exposed risk. The seven major millennium impact categories as shown in the following chart and in appendix B.

```
Millennium Impact Categories

1.  Personal Safety
2.  Government Services
3.  Utility & Infrastructure
4.  Communications and Computer
5.  Employment & Income security
6.  Banking & Finance
7.  Personal Assets and Electronics
```

Your personal preparedness plan can be built around the risk assessment checklists that are in appendix C and the mini-checklists that accompany the end of each of the following four chapters. The checklists use these millennium impact categories as an organizational framework that you can use to evaluate your own personal "supply-chain" to see how the things around you could possibly be affected during each of the four *millennium periods*.

As we explore the ramifications of each of the *millennium periods*, keep in mind the macro-economic viewpoint that is the basis for the forecasts and scenarios and realize that these kinds of occurrences are going to be widespread around the world. They don't need to happen in your town or in your backyard in order to affect your family, your business, and you. Many of these occurrences are like ripples in the water from which their damage spreads out across the landscape. The damage is spread through the supply-chain affecting the dependent entities, one by one. The entities that are prepared will be in the best position to cope and ultimately recover from whatever damage is presented. Those that are not prepared will be the entities that will be the next in the supply-chain to sustain damage. It then becomes a matter of viability and resilience whether that entity will survive or become another failure statistic standing in the long line of Y2K litigants.

Let us now examine the specific details of each *millennium period* and work towards building a plan to make sure that we will individually be a survivor and possibly ensure that the people around us are fast to recover from the millennium and its uncertain effects.

The Pre-Millennium Period (PMP)

As you may remember, the *PMP* is the period leading up to the end of November 1999. This is the time that will be marked by certain conflicting claims, hype and denial of the existence and/or the magnitude of the millennium problem. This is the best time for us to prepare for the other *millennium periods* because we can look ahead at our own pace, to the expected impact of the future, without the pressure of imminent panic. We want to get a jump on everyone else, so to speak. This is what planning is all about.

Each day that goes by since the 1st day of 1999 brings more and more news of the Y2K bug. There was even a news clip on CNN recently about the all the taxicab meters in Singapore stopped working at midnight on January 1, 1999. Is this a coincidence or is this a sign of the inconveniences to come? I will let you decide for yourself. The fact is that you should be building your personal preparedness plan as soon as you complete this chapter.

I have stated before, and it is worth repeating, that the *PMP* period is the most important time to make your decisions about how prepared that you will be. If you are going to make changes to your financial portfolio or open additional local bank accounts to ensure that you have backup cash and funds available, you need to be doing this prior to the beginning of 3rd quarter 1999. Why? Because once the *Hyper-Millennium Period* starts in late 3rd quarter, people are going to begin the panicked preparations. You need to have your preparations complete in order to avoid the inconvenience and possible personal danger that can be encountered in later time periods.

How do I know this? Do you remember back in 1988 when the now infamous climatologist, Ivan Browning, made the prediction that there would be a major earthquake striking the middle section of the US along the new-Madrid fault on or around December 4th caused by lunar and planetary alignment? You may just barely remember this because it never happened as he predicted. The fact was that people didn't know if it would happen or not. They waited until the last several days before the prediction date and then jammed the stores clearing the shelves of bottled water, canned goods, candles, flashlights, and batteries. It was utter chaos. In fact, I was one of the ones in the grocery store the day before the prediction date. I speak from experience and with conviction saying to you; I will not live through that again! In terms of the "Earthquake Preparedness Continuum", I was clearly trapped on the right side of the chart. I waited until the last minute and reacted to the hype of the media talking about how bad it was going to be when the earthquake occurred. Rather than preparing in the months prior to the prediction date, I waited until the last minute like everyone else.

At the risk of sounding conservative, I humbly predict that a similar thing will happen regarding the millennium. People will listen to the stories and the hype and feel that they can wait until much closer to the date before doing anything about it. It will take more than several publicized Y2K related failures that affect others to get many people to begin panic buying. That is just the American way and is just human nature for many people in a busy society.

It will be close to the beginning of third quarter of 1999 (October 1) before stories of major Y2K related failures start to trickle out from the press. Only then will people begin to take the threat seriously. The retail industry will be trying its hardest to keep people focused on the holiday shopping season and this, in effect, will mask the millennium coverage by the press and delay the onset of preparation of the masses until the last week or two before January 1, 2000.

Let us look at the checklist in appendix (C). I have built the checklist in the order of the seven-(7) millennium impact categories and listed the items in the order of importance for you. Let us take each category and the items in it. You will notice that for the *Pre-Millennium Period* (*PMP*), many of the items are marked "None" or "low" because in many cases, life will continue on as usual for most areas of people's life until the *Hyper-Millennium Period* and the subsequent *millennium periods*. It is actually in the *HMP* and the *CTMP* that many of these items on the list become critical. The part of this checklist that you must concentrate on in this period is the risk assessment section. The *PMP* is the planning stage so it is here that you must begin to take the steps laid out in the checklist in the appendix and listed at the end of this chapter. Many of the sample categories have been completed for you, but you should add categories that apply to your personal situation.

In the *Personal Preparation and Safety* category, let us look at some of the items on the list. Regarding safety, there would be little threat to your personal safety at this time, nor would there be a threat to your shelter, medical, food, or water. However, it is during this period that it starts to make sense to build reserves of some of these items to make sure that they are available when you need them. You might consider setting aside an area in your home or living quarters to store emergency rations of canned, non-perishable food, bottled water, medicine, extra blankets, candles, flashlights, and a supply of emergency cash. How much you might ask? From all of the information I have been able to gather, I believe that the highest probability of service disruption to any particular location would last several days to a week. As we have discussed, no one really knows for sure how long these might last or if they will even strike your area. There could be no disruption in your location or there could be a local power outage that could last weeks. I am only recommending that you assess your own risk level and make preparations accordingly. This risk assessment must include investi-gation of your personal supply-chain to determine in what areas you are exposed. If your electric company is progressive with its Y2K related preparations and announces that there will be no problem with electricity supply at the millennium, then you are lucky. I would consider having electricity and natural gas for heating some of the basics that would make the millennium an event rather than a disaster. That is good for you, but rest assured that there will be some people reading this book that will not be so fortunate. Consider electricity to be a fundamental element because without it, every-thing including remediation of the Y2K related causal factors will become dramati-cally more serious.

Regarding *personal transportation*, there should be no effect on this category during this period. There could be a temporary effect in the subsequent periods if there is disruption to the supply-chain of gasoline, diesel fuel, oil, refining chemicals, pipelines, or the pumping mechanisms that get the fuel from the oil well to you. You might want to consider a personal reserve of 10 gallons of gas stored safely in a 5-gallon gaso-line can obtainable from your local discount store. If you don't need it, you can always pour it in your automobile or lawnmower later.

Regarding *asset protection*, again there is no immediate impact in this period because it is before any of the Y2K related effects are set to occur. Regarding *travel plans*, the decision is up to you, but are you willing to take the financial and potential safety risk of scheduling a vacation or trip that crosses the *millennium period*? We discussed before that there could be a drastic reduction in air traffic control imposed by the Federal Avia-tion Administration because of the age of the computers that control radar and air traffic and the uncertainty as to air traffic safety. If you are booking a trip now for the future, then you might want to consider a trip that returns before the millennium date. If the trip is for the year 2000 and beyond, you may want to consider waiting until January or February and booking it only after you are convinced that the dangers have passed and you can make your journey and return without an unexpected disruption.

In the major category of *Government Services*, there is little impact expected during the *Pre-Millennium Period* and there is not much that you can do to prepare except investigate the government's plan to continue the delivery of the services that you depend upon and plan accordingly. Retired and elderly citizens will find that they depend upon the government far more than many other citizens. According to a press release that was published on CNN recently, the Social Security Administration was one of the most prepared government agencies. That is good news for many Americans who depend upon this for their subsistence. The bad news is that the Department of Energy, the Department of Defense, and the Department of Labor lagged far behind many other organizations and received barely passing grades by the Government Accounting Office (GAO) for Y2K related preparation. Reports have been circulated that the government will issue subsistence checks and electronic transfers before January 1, 2000 to ensure that there is no disruption in financial service to those who depend upon it.

Considering *Utility & Infrastructure* as a category, there is little risk in the *Pre-Millennium Period* (*PMP*). Most of the risks associated with this category will occur at the millennium transition and thereafter. I would encourage you to take the time during the *PMP* to research your utility companies and determine what plans they have for the millennium passage. We talked earlier about the electric and natural gas supply companies and how important their readiness will be to everything else. If you are not satisfied with their answers to your questions and inquiries, then you can ask your public service commission in your state or country to obtain the information for you. There are typically government agencies that watch over utilities to make sure that they treat the public fairly. They will probably be able to get a Y2K readiness report from the utilities that you are concerned about. They may even publish a document or have a web site that contains Y2K readiness information about your local utilities that you can review.

Regarding the major category of *Employment & Income security* the risk of a failure during this period is relatively low, but now is the time for you to build your preparation plan before it is too late. Many people in the world today live month to month for a variety of reasons. Any disruption to their subsistence or paycheck could prove devastating. Financial planners have long suggested the wisdom of having a liquid savings reserve equal to 3–6 months of income that one can use in the event of an emergency or loss of income. Few people that will be reading this book can honestly answer that they have heeded that advice. That is the reality of the world today. It does not take a potential world crisis event like the Y2K to remind us how important it is to follow this advice. Let me recommend that you spend whatever time you have available during the *Pre-Millennium Period* and start setting aside some reserve funds, gradually and subtly. In the event that your employer is adversely affected by the Y2K, or is somehow affected by a supplier-chain failure that disrupts the business, either temporarily or otherwise, you may find yourself without that monthly paycheck that you need to live.

You should also take an opportunity to review the method by which your income is received from your employer. Many people still use the manual paycheck delivery method. That means that they have a check cut and it arrives at the workplace or in the mail and it is then taken to the bank and manually deposited. Other people use electronic deposit of their funds directly into their bank accounts. Now is the time to review this process as a way to minimize your personal risk and set about any changes that are necessary to ensure a continual flow of funds in the event of service disruption at the millennium transition. In an upcoming section, we will discuss the wisdom of opening multiple bank accounts at different local banks so that you have a backup in the event of a failure at your other bank. If your employer allows for electronic fund deposit, you can specify that the funds are deposited divided across several institution destinations. You might also consider specifying that a certain small amount is cut on a manual check as well as the funds that go to the banks. That way, you have built a contingency plan that will get funds to you using several different paths. The same type of contingency planning and diversification can be used for IRA, Pension, and 401K fund withdrawals that you may be entitled to.

I include the category of *scams and fraud* as an item that needs to be addressed now even though the likelihood of it occurring during the *PMP* is relatively low. I urge you to be on your guard because there will be a host of scams associated with the Y2K that will be unleashed on the innocent and unsuspecting citizen. Be extremely careful with special investment schemes and Y2K related preparation packages and programs that will become available. If they are too good to be true, they just might be. As long as there have been humans on this planet, there have been those who take advantage of the unsuspecting, especially during calamities or periods of panic. Use the Internet, the Better Business Bureau (BBB), and second opinions to help you assess these ideas before it is too late.

Regarding the major category of *Communications and Computer*, this is an area that needs to be addressed during the *PMP*. There are things that you can do to investigate and prepare your computer equipment and software so that it is *Y2K ready*. The actual task that you will perform will vary depending upon which computer and operating system that you have. It has been reported recently that even Microsoft Windows 98 needs a special software "patch" downloaded from their website to ensure Y2K compliance. If you have any other version of Microsoft Windows such as 3.1 or Windows 95, you must assume that you need to do something in order to guard yourself from the Y2K bug. Windows NT version 4.5 and greater, most recent UNIX operating systems, and LINUX the operating system are reportedly compliant, but you should be careful to verify the specific version down to the decimal place of the version model number with the manufacturer in order to be completely sure. The *PMP* is the right time to perform the investigation and testing to be sure. The time to be testing is not the week before the millennium date because you will have no time left to determine a remedy if you find a condition that is unacceptable.

Once you determine that your operating system and the computer itself is compliant, it is time to determine the condition of the other software that resides and runs on your computer. One of the most basic ways to determine this is to inventory what software is running or is loaded on the computer and verify the software model and serial numbers against the manufacturer information that is available through their customer service phone numbers or through their web site. You can also attempt to test the software by running an actual simulation by setting the computer time and date ahead so that the computer and the software running on it thinks that it is already January 2000. Remember that there are three different millennium time events that you must be concerned with. The software's ability to deal with the time and date at exactly 12:00 on January 1, 2000; the time and date after it is year 2000; and the computer's ability to deal with leap year (February 29, 2000). After you test all of these conditions, you can be pretty well certain that you have resolved the year 2000 issues on your personal computer in the state that it is in. Any subsequent installation of software including downloads from the Internet reintroduces risk back into your computer world. Considering this, you can see why it has become such a monumental task for corporations and government organizations around the world to prepare for the millennium passage. You can also see why many organizations have issued a moratorium on new software being introduced onto organizational computers and networks after particular "freeze dates" in 1999.

Once you have determined that your personal computer is compliant, it is time to address the other areas that computers can touch your life. Risk of Billing/Accounting Errors is probably the least likely to occur during this millennium phase. The most risk will occur as the December 31 date gets closer because the calculations used to formulate the billing and accounting begins to encroach the actual millennium date period where most of the potential errors will occur. I would, however, begin to look closely at all of your bills and statements more and more closely anytime after July 1999. Look especially close at interest and finance charge calculations, especially at ones that have an accrued interest feature that crosses the millennium.

It is also advisable to examine balance due and amortization schedules closely. Take a sampling of the last statement and compare for accuracy. It would be helpful for you to conduct month to month analysis of each of your accounts by creating a simple chart showing monthly payments, finance charges, interest, and balance due dates. Use this chart each month to make sure that there are no abnormalities as the bills come in. If you detect something out of place, contact customer service as soon as possible to get an explanation. Just because something appears wrong doesn't necessarily mean that you have been the victim of a Y2K related failure, but as the date draws near, the likelihood that the two events are related increases proportionally.

It would be advisable to prepay any of your consumer debts, loans, and mortgages, if possible. We will examine this area more closely as we look at the other *millennium periods*, but with impending economic strain and the probability of rising interest rates with the surge in demand for short term cash, it would be to your advantage to reduce or consolidate debt.

Many of your common telecommunication facilities such as telephone/fax/internet, cellular phone Long Distance Carriers, and other related services should remain relatively unaffected during the *PMP* period.

One of the areas that stand to benefit immensely from advance planning and preparation is banking & finance. This is one of the areas that will affect American citizens the most throughout the entire ordeal as I anticipate there to be economic turmoil as a result of the Y2K related business failures resulting from supply-chain disruption. The problem is that the sword is double edged in that we can be affected both directly and indirectly by failures. Take a look at the volatile nature of the stock and bond markets during 1998 and in 1999, so far. Just the mere mention of negative aspects and the market swings wildly. Investor reactions to worldly events seems to be ever more pronounced. In just the past 18 months, we have seen events such as the Asian financial crisis, and fears of inflation or deflation in south American countries and other factors cited for record breaking swings in the stock and bond market indexes. The possibility of changes in the federal reserve rate, and reactions to comments about the economy by Alan Greenspan, the chairman of the US Federal Reserve Bank, have also had large psychological affects on the markets.

What we can learn from these events and the many similar distressful events throughout the past 75 years is that the market and thus our relative wealth is driven by intangible, sometimes irrational factors. Mood swings that tend to drive commodity prices in the financial markets are fueled by the general and financial press and news media reports about certain topics that investors perceive to have future impact on corporate earnings and investment performance. The Y2K is certain to be one of the cases that history will look at as one of those market drivers. What we need to address is how to safeguard ourselves in the likely event that investors panic at the onset of the millennium or, worse yet, panic at the occurrence of actual bank and business failures during or subsequent to the millennium passage. Some of these failures could be domestic, but more than likely, the trigger event will originate in foreign countries and then cause "supply-chain" failures that affect the American and the global economic balance.

From a *Pre-Millennium Period* perspective, we must take a proactive planning and preparation approach to this entire financial area. This is the time that we need to examine our personal, professional, and business portfolios. We must make a conscious decision about how to reallocate our assets to properly safeguard our financial investments.

If you look at the way that many investment advisors have guided us toward investment allocation, we see a typical spread of assets consisting of 25% aggressive growth 50% moderate equity and income securities, and 25% bonds and other stable financial instruments. Over the past 50 years, this mix has stood the test of time to be the best performance and the most able to withstand fluctuations in the local and global economies. Especially lately with the onslaught of the "day traders" using on-line trading and instantaneous information sources such as E*Trade and CNBC, we have seen huge amounts of new capital pouring into the financial markets. This has skewed the long-time allocation of portfolios shown above to closer to 70% stocks and stock funds and 30% bond and stable instruments. In this new mix, investors have pushed their portfolio mixes out to 30–35% aggressive growth company stocks. These, such as the web stocks that are so popular now are the small-cap stocks and technology companies that could be most adversely affected by a rapid and prolonged contraction of market capitalization.

Even though with the way that the market has yielded unprecedented market returns for investors, should we not rethink this mix of our market portfolios for a 6 to 12 month period beginning in mid 1999? What if we could anticipate a market downturn or cautionary disturbance related to the Y2K and reallocate our resources to take advantage of this? What I am suggesting is that starting in 4th quarter 1999, the public at large will begin to analyze the possible effects of a Y2K related surge of small and medium business failures caused by direct and indirect Y2K related failures. This will lead to an escalating degree of market contraction as people, especially smaller investors, begin to move their moneys out of stocks and into bonds or even out of the market entirely. This has a self-fulfilling effect as businesses begin to fail as their lifeblood capitalization begins to contract. In a recent meeting with representatives from a major brokerage house, it was reported that they have already witnessed major investors pulling accounts as large as $5 million stating that they are just to nervous about the direction the market is heading over the next 12-months. What do these investors know that the rest of us should be paying attention to?

Please note that I do not advocate wholesale shifts of accounts out of the financial markets. It is this very aspect, collapse of investor's confidence in the financial markets after an extended period of aggressive, over-optimistic buying, that contributed to the great depression in 1929. I recommend that you consult with your financial advisor or a qualified broker prior to performing any reallocation of your portfolio. Remember that you could incur sales and commission charges when exchanging securities or mutual fund shares. Do not create a liability for yourself in the process of trying to balance out your portfolio diversity.

I see this occurring through at least first to possibly second quarter of the year 2000 before people begin to move discretionary funds back into the market. This is a very important concept. It is also a chicken and the egg scenario because the preparation step advocated here is to consider a reallocation of your portfolio that minimizes investments in the sectors most likely to be affected by the any psychological correction or Y2K itself. Anticipate the market movements and beat the general public by investing in the blue chip companies of the market sectors when they are down and ride them back to health.

What I would suggest to you, if you believe these facts to be true, is to enact a slow and subtle shift in your funds of your portfolio beginning in July 1999. If you have large amounts of money in mutual funds such as 401K plans, then moving into related funds with different market focuses should not cost you anything more than a call to the 800 number or some quick changes on the website. It will be harder for those with large stock portfolios to make these types of shifts due to the capital gains taxes and the commissions that would be paid to brokers in order to initiate such changes. If you are holding shares of blue chip companies such as IBM, EXXON, Microsoft, Dupont and others, than you may want to just hold on. The people, I believe that are most at risk are the inexperienced individual investors who have skewed their port-folios toward the highly leveraged technology stocks and so called "small-cap" compa-nies. I do not believe that the current trend toward technology will dissipate, but I do anticipate that it will slow down long enough to watch the fireworks of the millen-nium. Investors will want to determine which companies will survive and which will not, and invest accordingly.

In order to protect your assets from rapid shrinkage, I would suggest that you consider a temporary portfolio strategy of 40% blue chip stocks and funds and 60% bonds, bond funds, equity instruments, and perhaps appreciating negotiable instruments such as precious metals including Gold, Silver, platinum, and the like. By reallocating your portfolio in this fashion, you may be reducing your overall returns for that period to single digits, but you will have less of an overall market exposure should the Y2K and its related havoc create turmoil in the financial markets. You can then revisit your invest-ment strategy as the smoke of the millennium begins to clear and you can determine which companies will survive. It just may be that new companies and new products emerge as the new leaders replacing some of the old guard that were not ready to move to the next century.

Whether you reallocate your portfolio or not, it is important that you take steps to safe-guard your important documents. I would advise that the *Pre-Millennium Period* is the time to organize, copy, and store all of your important financial and legal docu-ments. This would include insurance policies, retirement plans, stocks and bonds, corpo-rate option grants, wills and real estate documents. If you do not hold your own certificates such as stocks, your broker will provide you with copies of them for your records. I have been told by at least one brokerage house that they have instructed their brokers to honor all such requests as they anticipate a huge rush of such requests as December 31, 1999 draws near.

I would also advise making copies of all bills and statements including investment accounts, credit card accounts, retirement plans, and bank accounts on a quarterly basis. I would take the opportunity, especially with the October 1 statements, to establish a base line for which to compare the December and March quarterly statements. It is these statements that I would expect the highest probability of errors. The easiest source of comparative data will be your September quarterly statements. By the time that the December quarterly statements run, it will be well into January 2000 and any errors will have the company swamped with computer and account repair work. Take advantage of the opportunity to prepay any January bills in November and December to make sure that your account is prepaid for January. This will avoid considerable frustration trying to get customer services attention trying to resolve billing errors and problems at the turn of the century.

The *Pre-Millennium Period* does not pose much of a threat to many of the aspects of our lives. This phase is one of preparation and for planning. Based upon the way that Americans live, this may prove to very difficult to do. The fact remains that this is the best time to do this kind of Y2K related preparation. It will become increasingly obvious that to beat the masses and the panic will prove a wise step.

The following is the risk and preparation summary chart for *the Pre-Millennium Period* sorted by millennium impact categories. The risks noted are arbitrary and subjective and represent relative risk, not absolute risk. The trend arrows represent the direction of risk movement from the last *millennium period*.

Pre-Millennium Period	Risk and Preparation Summary Chart		
Millennium Impact Category	**Risk Areas**	**Risk Trend**	**Preparation Areas**
Personal Safety	None	⇔	Identify risks, store emergency supplies of water, food, blankets, etc.
Government Services	None	⇔	Identify risks and supply-chain, get copies of SS account, resolve tax accounts
Utility & Infrastructure	None	⇔	Identify risks and supply-chain, Identify alternate sources of fuel, if possible
Communications and Computer	None	⇔	Identify risks and supply-chain, identify alternative sources, download all available Y2K software patches, test computer and software for Y2K readiness
Employment & Income security	None to Low	⇔	Diversify income sources, if possible; Examine your companies supply-chain upwards and downwards for risk
Banking & Finance	None to Low	⇑	Reallocate financial assets, investments, retirement accounts, 401K, etc.; Setup redundant financial accounts; Make copies of all statements; Prepay January bills in early December and get copies of statements; Payoff as many accounts as possible before holiday season; Holidays should be paid in cash, if possible
Personal Assets	None to Low	⇔	Test personal electronics for Y2K readiness;

The risk factors listed in the preceding chart are reference values only. They indicate relative risk factor for that *millennium period* and do not necessarily indicate whether a failure will occur and whether it will affect your family, your business, or you. It is important that you evaluate your own risk for that period and take appropriate action in terms of preparation and diversification, if applicable.

The following is the preparation checklist that you can use for the *Pre-Millennium Period* that summarizes the steps necessary to be ready. Review this chart frequently as this period approaches and add any new items that you download from the website *y2kbook.8m.com*.

Pre-Millennium Period
Preparation Checklist

❑ Investigate your supply-chain looking for risk
❑ Investigate your employer's, banks, government's, and infrastructure readiness and vulnerability for Y2K and determine if risk is acceptable
❑ Reallocate your financial portfolio for maximum conservative diversity, the same as for economic slowdown
❑ Start to reserve cash in small increments in a safe place
❑ Diversify your financial institutions early
❑ Don't be in a panic and cause more harm preparing by overreacting
❑ Avoid overreaction during your preparation by staying practical
❑ Payoff as many credit cards or revolving credit accounts as possible during the *PMP* to avoid rising interest rates as the millennium approaches
❑ Use a checklist and follow millennium impact categories to organize your preparations

---

The *Hyper-Millennium Period (HMP)*

The *Hyper-Millennium Period* is a one month period beginning approximately on November 30, 1999 and lasting right up until the last minute before midnight on December 31, 1999. There will probably be an increased number of Y2K related failures than will have occurred in the *Pre-Millennium Period*, that was just described. The possible failures will be related to certain programs that are run generating bills, statements, and invoices that cover or are due in January 2000.

The main distinction with this period will be the escalating preoccupation and analysis by the press of the negative aspects of the approaching millennium passage, fueling public reaction. This increasing and unrelenting press coverage will amount to a wake-up call for many Americans. At first, I believe that most people will focus only on the celebration of the coming event itself following the rush of millennium branding that will dominate television and radio. Slowly and steadily, people will begin to become emotionally stirred realizing that the news reports weren't exaggerated and that there will be some negative implications that just might affect them. This will begin to bring on random acts of irrational behavior both socially and financially.

Again you will find that this period will be marked by wild swings in the financial markets and predictions of various doom and gloom types being cast against those who preach "all is well, enjoy the party!"

The point is that this is the last opportunity for those who don't want to be "Y2K victims" have to get their preparations in order. I do not predict any major social or behavioral meltdowns, but rather what I see is a growing preoccupation with the event, and a growing financial system crisis caused by overreaction of people acting out of fear, uncertainty and doubt. I predict that many people will continue on business as usual until after the December holiday, then they will move into a "frenzy" propelled by press reports, hyped media coverage and "millennium" sales of every kind and description. The people who desire not to be a victim of Y2K will already have completed their preparations and will avoid most of this last minute madness and will concentrate on final preparations with their families, businesses, and their churches.

Refer again to the famed climatologist, Ivan Browning, and his prediction of a cataclysmic earthquake during December 1988. His conviction was so genuine that people for hundreds of miles around St. Louis and Memphis braced for the event. Finally, two days before the event, it seems that everyone rushed the stores. You could not find candles, shelf braces, bottled water, batteries, flashlights, and food anywhere. The lines were long and patience was short. Now twelve years later, most everyone affected by that close call with the disaster that never happened has long since let their memory of that nightmare slip away.

Does this event have anything to do with the coming millennium passage? I believe that it does. People will act the same way. They will talk about the event but, through denial, will postpone preparation until the last minute spurred by news reports of people standing in lines at grocery stores and ATMs two days before New Years 2000. Only this time, the effects will not be local like it was in 1988. Unlike Browning's prediction which many people, including his peers, disputed until that very day, few people including the experts doubt the probability of problems and disruptions that will be caused by the Y2K bug. What they don't know is how hard it will hit and what effect it will have upon our local, national, and global societies.

In February 1999, it was reported in USA Today that the Internal Revenue Service admits that after spending $1 billion dollars on Y2K related testing and remediation that there would be problems with the tax collection and payment system. They know it and are admitting it 10 months ahead of time. This should serve as a curtain call for many of us who will surely postpone our belief and concern until the last minute, but it probably won't change the reality that most people will wait until late in the *HMP* to prepare.

We can be sure that if people all across the nation, and indeed around the world, react in anywhere near the way they acted in 1988 to the earthquake prediction, then we indeed have a problem that must be prepared for on a widespread personal basis.

In the *Pre-Millennium Period* we concentrated on preparation in the financial aspects because that was the area where we had the most to lose if we waited too long to start our preparation. In the *Hyper-Millennium Period* we must begin to concentrate on completing areas such as personal preparation, safety, and logistics, as well as the constant fine-tuning of our portfolio and the completion of our financial preparations.

What I advocate is to stay one step ahead of the masses of people who will begin to crowd the stores immediately after the 1999 holiday season trying to stock up on emergency supplies and visit their banks and financial institutions. We as prepared citizens determined not to be Y2K victims will have completed these steps weeks and even months before.

If we believe that we should stock up with water, firewood, food, candles, batteries, and flashlights as a way to have piece of mind in the event that the worst comes to pass, then let us not wait until the rush of the stores at the last minute. To do so could put us in possible personal jeopardy and inconvenience. The same holds true for getting spare cash. It is not unrealistic to believe that there could be a disruption in our ability to get funds from our banks and our ATM networks at the turn of the century. It is even more plausible to believe that everyone may get the same idea the last several days before January 1, 2000 spurred by media coverage of banking experts predicting cash shortages caused by people suddenly drawing large amounts of cash from their bank accounts. In reality, most cash will be relatively safe in our banks and credit unions, but it will be people's perception that it might not be that will cause the rush. The Federal Reserve has announced that it will increase the circulation of cash by infusing over $50 billion into the economy during the *millennium period* to cover the anticipated shortages that could arise. The problem is how to get this cash into peoples hands before it is absorbed into the global economy by countries who value our currency more than they value their own. The Federal Reserve has announced that they will make this new cash available in fourth quarter. I understand this to mean the federal fiscal 4th quarter that ends in September 1999.

This must be taken as a clue that the government believes that there is a risk to the money supply and they are reacting with a proactive measure as a way to stem unnecessary churning of bank accounts. How much cash should you put aside? Many experts agree that any inconvenience at the Y2K caused by power outages or ATM network failures can probably be resolved within several days to a week. I believe that having a stash for two weeks is plenty, but that depends upon you and your needs.

I would make the same recommendation for emergency supplies such as water, food, batteries for flashlights and radios, and the like. Remember this is going to be January! It could be very cold and the days are short. If there are power or utility supply-chain problems, it will become highly inconvenient for those affected. Again, I would suspect that power and utility problems are going to be scattered, if they strike at all. Most utility companies are doing their best right now to make sure that they are ready for the event. If problems or outages do occur, it will be due to unexpected problems in the power grid distribution and management equipment.

In the *Hyper-Millennium Period*, safety preparation will be a concern but actual safety problems are probably not going to come into play until the real rush begins after the Y2K related event causes hard failures. I am urging people to be very aware of possible scams or fraudulent schemes that may be at play. People will be trying to take advantage of other's fears by introducing special protection packages and the like. Be very wary of people offering to protect you or your assets for the Y2K event. Stay with blue chip companies, financial institutions, and organizations. If you are not sure, then contact the Better Business Bureau or the local police to find out before investing any money in unknown investments.

One of the areas that I want to caution you about is IRA, pension, and retirement fund withdrawals, especially in a period of reactionary panic like the *Hyper-Millennium Period* is sure to be. It is not prudent to try to remove your funds or prematurely cash them in. The financial system is quite secure as long as you have chosen a secure, blue chip Company or bank as your repository. Withdrawals by participants, even if temporary, will lead to government or institutional withdrawal penalties, taxable events, commissions of back loaded funds, and other charges that will unnecessarily erode your earning power for the future. You may be very tempted to pull your money to safety, especially in the *Hyper-Millennium Period* after hearing of all the pending doom and gloom, but you must resist this temptation. The strategy that you should use instead is reallocation of your assets within your fund families into safer or more solid investment categories. If your funds are invested across the standard 25%–50%–25% portfolio diversification range, then consider reallocating the upper most risky 25% into more stable bond funds or equity income categories, at least for several months or until the market calms back down after the millennium passage. This way you can feel secure that you have safeguarded your nest egg into a safe location that will last through the millennium change. If you have not reallocated your portfolios in the *Pre-Millennium Period* ending in November 1999, then now is the time to complete this step before interest rates begin to rise throwing the market into wild swings that can result in serious losses of principal.

One trap that many people I talk to fall into is to have most of their money allocated into one or two fund companies. In stable times this is fine, but in a time of approaching financial turmoil, I must recommend that you spread your assets across several fund companies, insurance companies, and banks. This will ensure to the highest degree possible that your future financial security will survive the millennium passage in tact and with a minimum loss of portfolio value.

I also recommend that people consider opening secondary bank accounts at major blue chip banks. We as a society have fallen into a state of confidence with the banking system and many of us use out of town banking institutions. This is probably still fine even with the millennium problem, but I recommend that you consider opening an account at a secondary financial institution located close to your home or business. If there is a temporary disruption in the power, communications, or ATM banking system, you want to have an alternative that is close so you have a source of funds until the rest of the banking system recovers from any difficulties in January or February 2000. Most banking experts to not expect there to be problems with their systems, especially in light of the pressure exerted on them from the Securities and Exchange Commission mandating "Y2K Readiness" by June 1999. Still, there are other problems that can arise along the supply-chain that can affect these institutions ability to serve you when you need service. Be prepared and diversify your financial holdings against several institutions.

Trying to open diversification and backup accounts the last week of December or after markets begin to fall in anticipation of possible business failures caused by Y2K will only lead to frustration on your part. Customer service lines and company web sites will be clogged with people panicking at the last minute. This is something that should be done by the beginning of the *Hyper-Millennium Period*, to avoid all possible frustration.

Once you have completed these steps, then it is time to sit back and watch the millennium approach and see what happens. What you will find is that you will either be glad you prepared as well as you did, or you will wish you prepared more. I feel pretty confident after all my research, that few will regret preparation or planning ahead for an event that is likely to change the way that many of us live our lives, if even for a short period.

The following is the risk and preparation summary chart for *the Hyper-Millennium Period* sorted by millennium impact categories. The risks noted are arbitrary and subjective and represent relative risk, not absolute risk. The trend arrows represent the direction of risk movement from the last *millennium period.*

Hyper-Millennium Period		**Risk and Preparation Summary Chart**	
Millennium Impact Category	**Risk Class**	**Risk Trend**	**Preparation Areas**
Personal Safety	Medium	⇑	Avoid risky situations and locations in latter part of period approaching millennium as hype and panic mount such as ATMs, grocery stores, etc.
Government Services	Low	⇑	
Utility & Infrastructure	Low	⇑	
Communications and Computer	Low	⇑	Set time and date past January 1 to avoid risk of millennium viruses and reduce risk of transitional problems,
Employment & Income security	Low	⇑	
Banking & Finance	Medium	⇑	Fine tune allocation of financial assets, investments, retirement accounts, 401K, etc. Prepay January bills in early December and get copies of statements; Make sure you have spare cash by early in period and avoid banks and ATMs in late period
Personal Assets	Low to Medium	⇑	Set electronic dates to after millennium to avoid transitional problems or viruses

The risk factors listed in the preceding chart are reference values only. They indicate relative risk factor for this *millennium period* and do not necessarily indicate whether a failure will occur and whether it will affect your family, your business, or you. It is important that you evaluate your own risk for this period and take appropriate action in terms of preparation and diversification in order to minimize risk exposure.

The next list is the preparation checklist that can be used to prepare and organize for the *Hyper-Millennium Period*. Review this chart frequently as this period approaches and add any new items that you download from the website *y2kbook.8m.com*.

Hyper-Millennium Period
Preparation Checklist

- ❑ Continue investigation of your supply-chain looking for risk
- ❑ Avoid risky situations such as banks and ATMs in last days of 1999 by preparing early and following your plan
- ❑ Have all your reserves of cash, food, grocery items, etc. stored early. Don't get stuck in long lines in final days of December 1999
- ❑ Don't be lulled into panic after holiday season
- ❑ Complete archiving of all bank, brokerage, retirement statements
- ❑ Pay bills, mortgages, lease payments, and other important accounts early (mid December 1999) if possible to ensure account credit prior to January 1, 1999
- ❑ Don't be in a panic and help to calm the people around you

---

The *Critical Transition Millennium Period (CTMP)*

So you have been planning and preparing for nearly three months for the event, now what? The world is sure to have plenty of festivities planned for the event and for many, the temptation to be a part of the excitement will prove to be too much. Despite their feelings that there might be certain inconveniences that could occur as a result, they want to enjoy the fun. That is fine, but let us first review some of the predictions and possibilities that could occur so that we know exactly how to minimize our risks, if we decide to venture out. Of all four of the *millennium periods* described and outlined in this book, by far this period will offer the highest probability of failures, financial difficulty, social upheaval, and general inconvenience. By far, the highest probability of failures immediately caused by the moment of millennium transition will be the time period immediately after midnight and the next several days into the first work-week of 2000. The exact period is not known, but in general, it will be until each particular failure can be addressed by the company's programming staffs and ultimately corrected.

Because January 1, 2000 is a Saturday, there is a distinct possibility that many errors and failures may go undiscovered until Monday, January 3. You will notice that the *CTMP* lasts until the end of March 2000. It is believed that it will take a full three months for many of the most damaging failures and Y2K related errors to manifest themselves and be either fixed or worked around by the managers and technicians that are responsible for them. It is further believed that the most devastating effects, the economic business failures caused by supply-chain failures will take months before their full extent is known.

As we have seen in our investigation of electronic and software devices in the previous chapter, there are several kinds of failures and several kinds of ways that software and devices will react at the millennium and the leap year shortly thereafter. These simple tests outlined in the last chapter and summarized in the appendix are the very crux of the entire threat to society. Every computer driven device that contains date and time dependent logic should be suspect until it can be tested and verified. The problem, as discussed early in this book is that there are literally billions of lines of software code embedded in everything from Corporate payroll systems to apartment building venti- lation and elevator control systems. We know that hundreds of thousands of these devices are installed all around the country and around the world. Many of these devices are old and in many cases out of production warranty. In other words, no one is addressing their function and their ability to withstand the Y2K event.

These very facts are what make the *CTMP* the most dangerous and volatile period of the millennium. The fact is that we know that things are going to go wrong, but we don't know which things and just how many there will be and just how society will be able to deal with them simultaneously. Think of the strain on Emergency services if elevators stopped working all around the country at the same time!

Let us go through the checklist again and look at the specific risks so that you can properly prepare for the wide range of challenges that you, your family, and your busi- ness will face.

One of the first areas we need to discuss is that of personal preparation and safety. Because there are likely going to be situations that will cause people to panic, this causes a destabilization in the behavior of many people who normally act with what we consider rationality. The safety threat to you and your family comes to play if you cross the path of one or more of these people in an irrational state. Consider the effect if you live in the city and the power goes out for an extended period. People cannot get into their buildings because the elevators do not work. Stores and restaurants are not open and people don't have anywhere to go. There have been times of power outages in big cities before. People tend to cope pretty well. Consider, though, the fact that this will be in the middle of winter when these failures will occur. Many people will be away from home at parties and New Years celebrations. If the power goes out then so does the mass transit systems (with the exception of buses). Many people may find themselves trapped in their locations away from their home comfort zone. If the power outage occurs, and it may or may not, then suddenly people begin to suffer panic. They may start to crowd into places to keep warm in an effort to seek shelter. You do not want to find yourself in a "mosh-pit" on New Years Eve.

Another area that I would advise that you consider avoiding is the use of elevators, at least for the first day of January 2000. Elevator control circuits are driven by computers and use a time and day function to determine car movement and placement algorithms. They are designed to park cars on the ground floors early in the morning and space out cars at specific floor levels near 5:00PM. In the event of power failures, these elevators could be stuck along with the people stuck in side them as the cars become confused on where to go. If the computers that control them fail, it is uncertain how they will react to the new millennium date now being fed to them as an input parameter. Most of these uncertainties should be clearer within the first day of year 2000. If the system doesn't fail on the first day, then chances are pretty good that they won't fail on the second day. Does this sound a little paranoid? I was once stuck in an elevator and I choose not to do that again. The final decision is yours but I will avoid elevators until after I am certain that they will operate correctly.

One area that must be carefully considered is that of travel. I mentioned earlier that there are concerns on the part of the FAA about the state of their relatively obsolete Air Traffic Control Radar system. If the FAA implements a precautionary Air Traffic Control flight restriction, as predicted, this could cancel or seriously delay thousands of flights each day. It is unknown how long the flight restrictions might last, but if you are out of town over the holidays you might get stranded or severely inconvenienced trying to get home. I would advise you to at least make sure that if you travel that you receive paper tickets and avoid "E-Tickets". Paper tickets can at least be bartered with other airlines in the event that your airline's systems have Y2K difficulty.

Am I suggesting that people not go out on New Years Eve to perhaps the largest public celebration that many people will ever witness? Not hardly, but you may be correct in assuming that I would recommend caution in your choice of locations to do your celebration and how you get there. It is up to you regarding how much personal risk you are willing to take. supply-chain failures can strike in some unexpected places and some inconvenient times.

The fact is that even the power industry cannot guarantee us that they won't have power failures or "brown outs" resulting from variances in power demand versus supply. The farther you move away from the largest utility companies, the ones that most likely had the financial resources to test their computer and power monitoring systems for Y2K readiness, the higher your chances of encountering problems will be.

Where is an acceptable level of precaution for the celebration of this event? The question comes down to managing risks and contingencies in the event of a problem. I personally would opt for a ground floor celebration rather than one at the top of an office or hotel building. I would opt for one close to home, or close to where I parked a vehicle to get home. I would choose one in the United States or another industrialized nation rather than a third world country, or one that is known to have ignored the risk of Y2K until the last minute.

One of the signs that trouble is expected is the fact that many banks and brokerage houses have hired security firms to guard their location from hoards of people trying to gain access to their money and accounts. It was recently reported on *CNN Moneyline* that the Chicago Mercantile Futures traders are very concerned about potential cash availability in the event of Y2K related financial panic. The futures prices for short-term cash for the time period around the millennium have already started to rise in anticipation of a cash shortage. It was mentioned earlier that the Federal Reserve has responded with an announcement that they will circulate an additional $50 Billion in US currency to ward off that demand to protect short term interest rates. Think of the implications on money supply if 100 million people decide that they want to withdraw $300 from their banks to have extra cash on hand for the millennium, in case of ATM or bank failures. Although in plain figures, the extra circulation of $50 billion from the Fed should cover the spike in demand. The problem will be having the cash evenly distributed and accessible to where people can get it. This is why it was strongly recommended that cash withdrawals and financial asset reallocation occur during the *Pre-Millennium Period* and not during the *Hyper-Millennium Period*. It is when people can't get their money that panic will really escalates, and the risk of personal injury or harm mounts if you are in the wrong place at the wrong time.

At the risk of sounding a premature warning bell, let me remind the reader that my purpose is to offer guidance in your preparation for this event so that you are not an unnecessary or unwilling Y2K victim. I am not advising people to go out and buy a tent and bury food and guns in your country retreat, although I have talked to people who think that this is an appropriate response. However, your planning for your last several weeks of 1999 and your first several weeks of 2000 should include enough contingency planning to make sure that you have access to food, water, shelter, warmth, and medical needs to last at least for several days to a week. This means you should have renewed any medical prescriptions or stock up on anything that you know that you will need weeks in advance.

I would advise storing several days to even a week of bottled water in a safe and secure location. I would advise you also to stock up on non-perishable canned goods that can be used to feed you and your family for up to a week in the event that events get out of control in your town or city.

The same situation could possibly occur for gasoline and fuel oil. The potential problem of having people lining up to get extra gas in the last several days before the millennium because the news has hyped potential shortages due to pipeline and "supply-chain" shortages will lead to long lines, escalating prices and short tempers. I would recommend that the prepared people keep their auto and gas tanks full and fill up their plastic fuel containers around their homes. I would also advise people to make sure that their cooking grill propane canisters are full, as well. If you have kerosene heaters, get their tanks filled up as well. Even if the worse of the Y2K predictions does not come to pass, at least you will have this extra reserve fuel that you can pour into your car or recreation vehicle.

For the purposes of discussion, all government services are grouped and analyzed together. Government services, again, includes all interactions between local, state, and federal government agencies and entities. These entities provide services that range from taxation, public aid, and welfare to driver licensing, land management, and fiscal policy management. Judging from studies of the various reports that the government releases, the federal government has been earnestly working on the millennium problem by funneling billions of dollars toward testing efforts at the major federal agencies. Unfortunately, as discussed earlier, the effort may have been too little, too late. Agencies such as the Defense Department, the Department of Energy, and the Department of Labor all received poor grades for their readiness posture as of a January 1, 1999 report published in USA Today.

The result of this lack of readiness at the federal level, to say nothing about the status of states and local governments, leaves it quite unclear as to the level of service disruption during the *Critical Transition Millennium Period*. As with many other aspects of the Y2K related threat, the disruptions will tend to be financial in nature such as taxes, public aid, welfare, food stamps, unemployment, social security, and budget and fiscal management. The exceptions are issues related to defense, space and satellite tracking, database-related management, and nuclear powerplant regulation efforts.

Everyone in the government has expended great efforts to thoroughly test every possible system, report, database, interface, fund transfer, and missile launch and tracking function. The fact is that it only takes several strategic errors to affect millions of people. The advice for the citizens of not only our country, but also every country that uses the Gregorian based calendar, is to prepare for service disruption for at least a period of time. People must prepare themselves by expecting that their entitlement checks or electronic transfers might be delayed or be in error. This is easier said than done. The truth of the matter is that delays and service disruptions are inevitable. People should be prepared for inconveniences lasting anywhere from several hours to several weeks until some of these functions are restored or a system for contingency is worked out or implemented.

Regarding air travel and other aspects of public transportation. The service disruptions are going to be caused by indirect failures rather than direct ones. Even though the Department of Transportation is intimately involved in areas such as air traffic control, Interstate commerce and vehicular safety, the systems that stand the most risk of failure are the power related systems which feed the computers that help this agencies do their work.

I recently attended a function sponsored by the Federal Aviation Administration and I asked the usual questions about Y2K readiness of their agency. The FAA administrator at this meeting told me that the FAA considers its Y2K testing effort complete and expects all systems to be ready by April 1999. They did not expect any other problems to be discovered nor did they expect any problems at Y2K. Although I was glad to hear this news, I remain somewhat skeptical that things are under control to the degree that it was stated. What this administrator may not be considering, nor the people who provided him the data that he was relaying at this meeting, was the risk of supply-chain failures.

Remember that supply-chain refers to the entire sequence of information, inputs, labor, or raw materials necessary to produce and deliver a product or service. It is the supply-chain failures that I remain the most worried about when I deal with any government entity. Most agencies within the government use a network of mainframe computers interconnected through complex programmatic interfaces to share information that feeds systems in other agencies. We mentioned before the interconnections that the IRS to Social Security, Social Services, Welfare records, and connections to most states computer systems. At some point, one of the data feeds coming to it might come from a private source such as a credit bureau or corporate payroll department. All it takes is for one of these feed systems to introduce a Y2K related failure or Y2K corrupt data into an otherwise sterile Y2K system and the whole system is now broken again.

Another example would be the Federal Aviation Administration (FAA) computers have ties to the National Transportation Safety Board, the Armed Services Personnel Center, Social Security, and the Department of Transportation mainframe computers. It also has an interface with the National Drivers License Registry Database to track driving infractions that is administered by a private company. If any one of these links introduces a failure or otherwise corrupt data, the whole system becomes unstable or suspect, despite all the preparations that may have taken place.

The only way that we will know for sure what will happen to the government provided services and entitlement programs is to actually experience the Y2K event first hand and see what breaks and fix it on a case by case basis. In the mean time, these agencies should be exhausting every possible means to thoroughly test every one of their systems and verify the validity of the systems supply-chains.

One possible effect of the actual millennium passage and the days and weeks that follow it will be the availability of police and fire protection and the continued availability of emergency services. I would not worry about a direct failure of the systems that support these services. I would worry about their ability to keep up with the spike in demand that will result from the sudden, short-term upheaval of some aspects of our social system as a result of panic or actual failures. This most likely to occur in the first several days to possibly weeks of the year 2000 as a result of peoples inability to get their money, food, supplies, or get to their homes as a result of utility or fuel pipeline failures.

The *Critical Transition Millennium Period* will be the time representative of the highest likelihood of disruption of utilities and utility infrastructure. Remember that all of our water, power, sanitation, heat/cooling, and natural gas are supplied and delivered by private companies. These systems all depend upon time and date sensitive computer systems to regulate flow based upon demand and to bill for measured services rendered per a unit of time. Some of the systems control only billing, others control the actual regulation and delivery of the product or service along its supply-chain to its ultimate destination. Once again, even though the companies themselves may be actively working on the Y2K related testing effort, they will not be able to guarantee the accuracy of the computer system interfaces of the suppliers in their supply-chain. This is important because the availability of electricity, food, water, and fuel has become an absolute necessity in our modern world.

Recall again the 12-hour blackout in San Francisco that resulted from an overloaded transformer at a power grid substation in late 1998. The newspapers were reporting chaos and gridlock in the city for that day period because people couldn't get to work and many couldn't get back into their apartment buildings. They simply had no where to go. Imagine a widespread failure that affected areas all across the country and even the world. What if this problem persisted for days or even a week waiting until crews could repair the systems that caused the failure? How would society in general cope with a situation like this? This is the precarious nature of the Y2K failure itself. We simply don't know the extent to which it can affect our complex interrelated world.

Hearing reports from the utilities that things are under control and they don't expect failures after midnight is not enough to take away my concern, nor should it you. Again, we must focus on solutions otherwise we become part of the problem ourselves. The solution is preparation that each of us should have put in place during the earlier stages of the *millennium periods*. We may not be able to stop the power from being interrupted during the first week of the millennium, but we can make sure that if it does, we are prepared enough that we are not inconvenienced, or worse, stranded.

We discussed earlier the impact that the millennium will have on employment and income security. Statistics reported in the USA Today in February 1999 reported that fully 68% of people polled expressed some concern that the Y2K event would affect them personally or professionally. Another statistic reported on ABC News on March 15, 1999 suggested that nearly 20% of people polled expected serious implications resulting from Y2K failures and a full 10% reported expecting a serious impact to affect them personally. These are amazingly high statistics for a period that is 10 months ahead of the event itself. This number, I would expect, will continue to grow throughout 1999 and will reach its peak during December 1999. I wish I had the background of the survey and knew both the questions that were asked and the target audience that were asked the questions. Because I don't, I must speculate on their concerns. It is fair to state that most people aren't yet aware of the complete ramifications of the event such as supply-chain concerns. They only know what they have heard and read so far. People are beginning to feel that there is a "hidden enemy" lurking around the corner that could effect the way they live and the way that they make their living. What needs to happen is that these people must be educated to properly prepare for the event to make sure that they are ready for any disruption that occurs. One such disruption will possibly be the employment of hundreds of thousands of people affected by business failures related to supply-chain failures.

Let us look at an example. I have talked to at least 5 major corporations in the last month who have announced that all computer related application development work will be terminated by September 1999. This work will not resume until after it is ensured that it is safe to continue the implementation of new computer applications for their business. In other words, these companies want to stabilize their computer systems for the Y2K and are not willing to risk the introduction of new problems into an already tested and sterile computer environment. Nobody can blame or take exception to this rationale to try to protect their organization from harm. The problem is that there are thousands of people whose job could be adversely affected because of this work slow down. People such as consultants, computer operations people, systems programmers, Software companies who sell software for application development, testing, and consulting services may all be adversely affected. The upside is that after January 1 passes and after February 29, 2000 passes then there will be an incredible pent-up demand for these services and the pendulum will swing back the other way. But for the people who depend upon employment and income from this industry, the effects may be devastating during the last two quarters of 1999.

Another area that is indirectly related is that of paycheck delivery method and electronic deposit. It is quite possible that the electronic commerce system that has become so prominent in our country and many others will be adversely affected by a Y2K related failure during the *Critical Transition Millennium Period.* Many of us have become accustomed to our paychecks being automatically deposited into our accounts by our employers. What if this system suffers a failure? Are we comfortable with our income floating aimlessly in cyberspace? What if the Payroll Company reports that the funds were transferred successfully, but our local bank suffers a failure and cannot reconcile the transaction and fails to report the successful deposit and availability of funds into our account?

There are a number of things that we can do to minimize the risk of this kind of failure. You will remember earlier that it was recommended that people open a secondary bank account at a large, local office bank so that we split up our liquid cash for the *millennium period* to ensure cash availability. We can also ask our employers to split up our cash transfers from our paychecks across these accounts. Perhaps it makes sense to split the transfer up for 70% of our income and receive the remaining 30% in a check in the mail. By doing this, even for a three or four month period, we have diversified our exposure so that the chances of receiving no income during the *CTMP* are minimal. I must urge you if you are considering this option, start early. It typically takes at least one to two payroll periods to make a change to an electronic transfer order. If you want the change to take effect in October paychecks, you should submit your paperwork in early September to beat the rush and make sure that the new arrangement works before January 2000.

Certainly, the most important risk during this period is to make sure that we have employment to receive a paycheck from. The people who are affected by secondary and economic related business failures or layoffs would have far more problems than trying to find lost funds from an electronic transfer. Although people feel there isn't much they can do to protect themselves from economic slowdowns or layoffs, they can attempt to reserve savings so that in the event that they are temporarily idled, they will have funds to hold them over.

Some of the same logic applies if you depend upon IRA, pension, fund withdrawals, or electronic transfer from other sources. Plan ahead. Diversify your holdings across multiple bank accounts, and ensure that you have adequate savings set aside in case of a fund delivery disruption in January or February 2000. Most funds and annuities provide for electronic transfers directly into your bank accounts. The risk exists that some of the transfers will be delayed or rejected due to failures on either end of the electronic transfer or electronic confirmation.

There is a risk that there will be a service disruption in communications and computer systems that we depend upon and have come to take for granted. The single largest error that most of us will encounter will be in the area of billing and accounting errors with the companies that we interact with. I fully expect that during the *CTMP*, at least 50% of us will be faced with some type of billing or accounting error that we must resolve somehow. Most of these errors will not show up until our January, February or March invoices and bills, but you can rest assured that there will be plenty of these errors to go around. Remember to look very closely at all statements and invoices that you receive and compare them closely with the invoices and statements saved from previous bills and statements.

Be especially wary of automatic debits from your account. This is a very popular feature for insurance companies to use. They are pre-authorized to withdraw a certain amount from your account on a specific day of every month. If these companies suffer some type of Y2K related anomaly; this could cause them to debit the incorrect amount from your account. If you are nervous about this possibility, withdraw the authorization for several months or consider a prepayment for the first quarter of 2000. Explain exactly why you want this to these companies and don't accept their attempts to convince you otherwise. This method of bill payment is normally highly reliable, but may be too risky during the *CTMP*.

Concerning personal computer software, I would advise leaving your computer turned off until January 1, 2000 arrives. As we discussed in the chapter on testing of devices and software, some devices and software may function sufficiently with the new millennium year but may suffer difficulty at the stroke of midnight. I am also wary of computer viruses that may be spread on the Internet that will prey on computers at the millennium. As a precaution or until you are certain that it is safe, consider resetting the clock and date on your computer back to 1998 for a short period of time. Watch and see what happens. If several days into 2000 there are no major reports of computer viruses or software crashes, then reset your computer clock and date to the correct date in 2000. Most of us with computers at home do not have critical applications that perform complex calculations based upon the computer system clock. The possible exception is bill payment and personal asset management software such as Microsoft Money and *Intuit's* Quicken. These software programs watch the systems time and date and issue reminder messages to the Windows "system tray" telling the user that they have bills due. Most of the US population is not affected by this problem because less than 1% of bank account holders utilize PC Banking integrated with bill pay services. What I would advise for anyone affected by this type of service is to order your software to pay all of your January bills during December, even if the amount paid is an estimate of the billing amount. That will allow the vendor or service provider to update their records with payment prior to January 1, 2000. This gives you the comfort of knowing that they have a whole month to straighten out their systems and the accounts of people who did not adequately prepare for Y2K related problems during January 2000.

I am asked quite frequently about whether the Y2K bug will affect other aspects of telecommunications such as local telephone service, cellular phone service, long distance carrier service, and Internet access providers. The answer is that we don't know exactly what the impact will be. I have had numerous discussions with local and long distance carrier companies who are working diligently on ensuring the reliability of their networks and switches for the *millennium period*. Most are reporting that their systems are now, or will soon be ready for the Y2K. All other aspects of our telecommunications infrastructure depend upon a handful of companies and their ability to withstand the pressures of the *Critical Transition Millennium Period*. If there are any problems with this telecommunications backbone concerning Y2K related problems, the rest of the system will suffer as well.

Cellular companies depend upon landlines that traverse through the switches, routers, and hubs of the local and long distance carriers. I would expect that the most error prone aspect of the system will be billing and collection based systems and their interfaces to the network switches. Remember that the foundation of our telecommunication billing system algorithm is time based. In other words, how many minutes did the service transaction last and what is the billing rate for that time of the day when the transaction took place? The good news is that a large percentage of our telecommunication companies are moving to flat-rate billing plans replacing the time of day and date based rate billing plans popular in earlier years. The complexity of the billing systems has decreased dramatically and, as a result, the reliance on time and date algorithms has decreased, as well. This increases the chances that the telecommunications companies can successfully complete the Y2K testing and systems corrections necessary to avoid major service disruptions during the *CTMP*.

One of the major areas that will affect many people during *this Critical Transition Millennium Period* will be banking and finance. I believe that the most serious impact to the general population will not be the direct Y2K related failures themselves, but rather will be the secondary business failures and economic impact that will result from them.

As you will recall, we talked about the importance of preparation during the *Pre-Millennium Period*. Hopefully, you have acknowledged the importance of investment allocation and important documents protection. If there are problems during the *CTMP*, your main recourse will be to have backup copies of all insurance policies, retirement plan contracts, copies of stocks and bonds, copies of all important documents. This should include bank and brokerage statements, backup bank accounts to diversify holdings, copies of all credit and debit card accounts, and taxes and tax accounts. Taking these steps will be key in minimizing the inconvenience you will suffer in reestablishing proper account balances and proper credit balances. I believe that this will preoccupy many of the transactions that take place during the first several months of 2000. Customer service phone lines and web sites will be congested with calls and inquiries about this very topic. I cannot guarantee that even with all of your diligence and preparation that you are not going to be one of the callers on the customer service lines trying to resolve credit and balance problems with your accounts. I do believe that your hard preparation work will payoff by minimizing the number of times that you have to do it to straighten out your overall portfolio.

We discussed the risk of failures of personal assets and personal electronics including computers and fax machines, etc. Hopefully, you have taken the time before the actual millennium passage to test your assets for Y2K susceptibility. If you have not, then you should minimize the risk to devices that depend upon date and time in their operational algorithms by resetting the dates of these devices back a year, or resetting them forward a year. The worse risk to many devices including computer operating systems and certain software will be at the stroke of midnight when the date first changes from 1999 to 2000. This is true for even the largest computers on the largest mainframes of our government and corporations. They may not have the luxury that you have to change the computer system clock and wait out the millennium passage to make sure that there are no large, unforecast problems.

In general, I believe that the area of personal electronics will be the least of your concerns. At least you can have piece of mind by knowing precisely whether your devices will pass or fail the Y2K event. My son told me that when he performed this test as I have just described on his VCR, it showed a day of "Thursday, January 1, 00" instead of Saturday, January 1, 00. The unit still worked, it was just the preset portion that no longer functioned correctly. In this case, the device has suffered a rather benign failure that will render the unit partially degraded after Y2K. This type of failure will only be an annoyance to many people.

The thing that most people need to focus in on is the preparation for the economic fallout and the indirect failures that are certain to occur as a result of the millennium event itself. I refer again back to the example of Ivan Browning's earthquake prediction because of the similarity with how I believe that people will prepare and react to this event. Remember that many people, including many of his own peers, disputed Ivan's prediction. The Y2K related event and its predicted fallout is doubted by few including the US government and major corporations across the country. Despite the fact that many international organizations have yet to react with the necessary seriousness, we should take serious the need for precautions for our personal safety and financial protection and needs that the large governmental and corporate organizations are. There is nothing wrong with stocking up some basic staples and essentials to last through this period of uncertainty. Just don't wait until the last minute or else you will have automatically become the victim.

The following is the risk and preparation summary chart for *the Critical Transition Millennium Period* sorted by millennium impact categories. The risks noted are arbi-

trary and subjective and represent relative risk, not absolute risk. The trend arrows represent the direction of risk movement from the last *millennium period.*

Critical Transition Millennium Period **Risk and Preparation Summary Chart**			
Millennium Impact Category	**Risk Class**	**Risk Trend**	**Preparation Areas**
Personal Safety	Medium	⇔	Avoid risky situations and locations in later part of the period approaching millennium as hype and panic mount; Avoid foreign countries, elevators, etc.
Government Services	Low to Medium	⇔	Possibility of reduced government services caused by high demand and Y2K failures of critical systems
Utility & Infrastructure	Low	⇔	Some risk of power outages and brownouts, other service interruptions should be temporary
Communications and Computer	Low to Medium	⇑	Risk of service interruptions, computer viruses, software date problems, set computers behind several days and see what happens
Employment & Income security	Low to Medium	⇑	Risk of business slow-downs or some early business failures caused by supply-chain problems
Banking & Finance	Medium to High	⇑	Fine tune allocation of financial assets, investments, retirement accounts, 401K, etc.
Personal Assets	Low	⇔	Any failures that will occur will occur right away, few will have a serious impact other than inconvenience

The risk factors listed in the preceding chart are reference values only. They indicate relative risk factor for this *millennium period* and do not necessarily indicate whether a failure will occur and whether it will affect your family, your business, or you. It is important that you evaluate your own risk for this period and take appropriate action in terms of preparation and diversification in order to minimize risk exposure.

The next list is the preparation checklist that can be used to prepare and organize for the *Critical Transition-Millennium Period*. Review this chart frequently as this period approaches and add any new items that you download from the website *y2kbook.8m.com* or other locations.

Critical Transition Millennium Period
<u>Preparation Checklist</u>

❑ Continue investigation of your supply-chain looking for risk and try to identify the failures or signs of failure as early as possible

❑ Avoid risky situations such as banks and ATMs in first days of 1999 by preparing early and following your plan

❑ Watch out for scams and fraud

❑ Don't get trapped somewhere where you can't get to safety if a direct failure or supply-chain failure occurs

❑ Make whatever adjustments are required with your financial institutions, banks, and brokerage accounts

❑ Don't be in a panic and help to calm the people around you

❑ Review any and all paycheck statements and credit account statements looking for errors

❑ Prepare letters to address account errors including copies of previous period statements as justification

❑ Use any means necessary to "as soon as possible" verify fund transfers, payroll transfers, etc. into the proper accounts

❑ Be prepared to switch to your alternate suppliers as soon as a supply-chain failure is detected. Catch problems immediately and resolve before everyone else does blocking access to customer service

---

The *Post-Transition Millennium Period (PTMP)*

The *Post-Transition Millennium Period* will begin in April 2000 and will last approximately a year ending in March of 2001. In general, most Y2K errors that anyone will encounter will occur during the *CTMP* that ends in March 2000, but there will be residual effects that will be felt by both shareholders and the economy at large for up to 15 months following January 1, 2000. There is a distinct possibility that some new errors will still occur as quarterly and earnings periods cross the millennium date may not be run until months after the millennium passage is past. There is also a possibility of secondary problems occur as databases containing some old 2-digit style dates are processed again for earnings reports, tax reports, and other once a year or once a quarter type transactions.

Initially the *PTMP* will be a period of upheaval and change as many of the business failures resulting from supply-chain failures occur and Y2K related litigation cases make their way through court. The PTMP will also become a period of healing and restoration. I would expect the economy and the financial system, that we know today, to continue on a slow road to recovery throughout the period. The thousands of Y2K related cases will make their way through the court system challenging many of the technology companies that have led the financial markets growth through the 1980's and 1990's. Smaller companies will challenge larger companies who put them out of business because of supply-chain failures and challenges.

When is all said and done, I would expect there to be anywhere from hundreds to possibly thousands of business failures that will result from either direct or supply-chain related problems stemming from the Y2K. Some of these will pose real challenges for the court system because of the drain they will place on resources of remaining viable companies seeking to defend themselves against Y2K related charges.

Some companies may have valid legal claims of consequential damage sustained as a result of suppliers who, out of their own negligence through lack of Y2K contingency planning, cut-off critical supplies of materials and/ or labor necessary to survive. There may also be viable consequential claims by smaller suppliers who were put out of business when they were unnecessarily cutout of the supply-chain by larger manufacturers seeking to diversify their vendors.

It was recently reported that the US Congress is considering a bill that would enact limitations on liability for Y2K related cases. We should be watching this carefully as it could set an important milestone and precedent for liability law. In either of the case types just mentioned, a law that restricts liability related to Y2K consequential damage will limit awards to companies that may rightly deserve them. In general though, it will tend to minimize trivial court cases and provide an overall shield on the economy. Considering the $1 trillion dollar price tag of liability estimated by the Government Accounting Office, anything that can help funnel viability back into the financial markets and the global economy rather than into legal defense funds and legal payrolls should be welcome. We want to encourage our legislators to act responsibly and ensure fair provisions are left in whatever Y2K Liability Limitations Act is placed into law. These provisions should include exclusions for fraud, willful misconduct, collusion, and other acts that can cause a company to suffer intentionally at the hands of another.

One question that needs to be addressed is: How will each of us be ultimately affected and how will we best move toward recovery of the confidence that we have in the world as we currently know it? This is almost as difficult of an issue to address as it is to specifically predict the Y2K related errors that will occur. Once again, preparation will be key to successful recovery.

Aside from situations that are totally out of our control, most of the situations that we will encounter will be ones that are inconveniences and can be overcome or worked around. If we did a good job of diversification of our personal and financial interests, then our impact during the *PTMP* will be largely minimal or nonexistent unless we are unfortunately related to a supply-chain failure or business that is adversely affected by one.

The underlying issue is the total impact on the economy of business failures and supply-chain failures that will inevitably occur? Some are making the assumption that the business failures will be mainly small companies and that their impact can be absorbed by an otherwise robust, and eager to move forward, financial market.

But how can we be sure? Remember that many aspects of the health of the economy are derived from consumer confidence and their willingness to buy goods and services. Every other aspect of the overall health of the economy itself can be affected by this factor as we have seen in the wild swings in the market indices during 1998 and 1999. The issue that needs to be addressed is that there may be a period of time that it will take consumers, and indeed businesses themselves, to recover from losses sustained during the *CTMP* and the *PTMP*. This aspect is one that the policy makers of our country, and every other country, must entertain now while there is still time to plan. They must not wait until next year at this time because they will be in the midst of the damage and will be forced to deal in a reactionary direction. The policy makers and economists must have contingency packages and plans that can be put in place to stimulate consumer and ultimately business confidence in the economy.

The problem is that we no longer live in a world that is just dominated by US interests. Indeed, as we learned with the Asian financial crisis in 1998 and 1999, things that happen outside of our country do have a direct impact on the way our country's economy works and operates. What will need to happen is that the healing that takes place in the *PTMP* must be truly global. All countries affected by the Y2K related problem must move forward together so that global economic health can be restored. Until this takes place, the foreign economies that were less prepared for the millennium passage will suffer larger, more devastating losses within their borders and those losses must be dealt with within our own borders and our own economy. Their losses become ours as the prices of commodities and products from other countries will remain unstable leading to edgy investors and commodity brokers keeping the US economy from fully recovering.

I believe that we must allow for a 12–15 month recovery period in our contingency planning for Y2K and its related effects. We simply don't know where the problems will strike and what the global and domestic effects on business will be thus leaving uncertainty about the consequences of personal implications. Because of this, we must allow for extra healing time to get things back to normal.

The fact is that the world has dealt with global crises before. Events such as World Wars I and II, the Cold War, and the problems in the Middle East have all presented challenges to the world and the economies of the constituent countries. The world eventually recovers and history has shown that it usually recovers for the better, but not without extreme hardship to thousands, and even millions, of people. We know that after the great World War, there was the "great depression". This was caused largely by a loss of consumer confidence in the banking and financial system as well as misguided protectionism. It was a perceived fear on the part of the millions of people who tried to pull their money out of banks and financial markets at the same time. Its implications were felt around the world, even in those days of isolationism. Today, we live in a nearly global economy and the impacts of major crises are felt nearly instantaneously in countries and economies around the world.

I would expect the fallout from the millennium event that will be observed during the *PTMP* to occur mainly in the financial, employment, and economic *millennium impact categories*. Referring back to the risk assessment chart outlined in Appendix C, most safety, infrastructure, utility, governmental, and personal asset impact risks will be reduced to a rating of low or minimal by the end of *the Critical Transition Millennium Period*. The ones that still remain are residual financial and economic problems resulting from surges in unemployment, business failures, Y2K related litigation, and market driven losses caused by dips in consumer confidence or Y2K driven market swings. It is important for our own well being that we anticipate these effects and manage our portfolios accordingly to maintain proactive diversification so that we do not suffer unnecessary losses.

The *PTMP* will be a period where dramatic changes could take place in the way that our world operates. It will be a time of growth and opportunity for many people and companies who properly prepared for the Y2K event and were lucky enough to escape contact with those entities that did not. I believe that new companies and new products will emerge that will reenergize the financial markets, especially the technology sectors. Those companies that show leadership and growth during the difficult millennium periods will become the leaders of the new century. You should be watching for signs of these companies' emergence and try to participate in their capitalization and market growth. Do this in an attempt to recover lost market value across your portfolio. I do not mean to suggest that the leaders of today's marketplace such as *IBM, Microsoft, Intel, Exxon, and Phillip Morris* will not be the leaders of the next century, because chances are that they will emerge in the new century still blue chip marketplace leaders. The point is that the *HMP* represents an opportunity for progressive companies to restore confidence to a market that will have been battered by fluctuating value and losses.

The issue that you must personally address as a result of reading this book is how to, through planning and preparation, alter your strategy to minimize the chances that you will encounter problems during the millennium transition. Anything that you can do to maximize your chances of millennium period survival should be explored.

The best advice that I can give you is to watch very closely around you and to spread out your risks of impact. Use every available piece of information that you can receive about known risks and make changes in your life or your circumstances to effectively minimize those risks to an acceptable level.

The changes in your portfolios and your routines should be evaluated for effectiveness before routinely changing back to the way things were in the *Pre-Millennium Period*. You may find that multiple and diversified bank accounts, diversified financial portfolios, and keeping your credit cards paid-off are policies that you want to continue into the new millennium. These changes are good. If these are the effects that reading this book and provoking thought will have, then it will have been a worthwhile time spent for me to have researched and recorded ideas that were helpful to you. In the presentations and consulting engagements I have participated in so far, it seems that most people believe that this is true.

The fact is that the millennium will change people's lives. Hopefully no one reading this text finds themselves an unwilling victim of a failed business or a scam. Perhaps you will find a renewed religious faith as a result of your experiences and the reflection on your live that you need to make in order to put these ideas into practice. Perhaps you will find that you are interested in political reform and decide to run for some political office. What ever the effect is, it most certainly will be realized during the *PTMP*. The fact is that many people will be so preoccupied during the *Critical Transition Millennium Period* reacting to the situations that occur that they will be unable to analyze the real impacts to their lives until months afterward. That is the true healing effect of the Hyper-Millennium Period and why it is designated to last a full year.

The following is the risk and preparation summary chart for *the Post-Transition Millennium Period* sorted by *millennium impact categories*. The risks noted are arbitrary and subjective and represent relative risk, not absolute risk. The trend arrows represent the direction of risk movement since the last *millennium period*. You will note that many of the risks are starting to decline as many parts of everyday life return to normal. Most mechanical related Y2K failures will have occurred and have been corrected.

Critical Transition Millennium Period **Risk and Preparation Summary Chart**			
Millennium Impact Category	**Risk Class**	**Risk Trend**	**Preparation Areas**
Personal Safety	Low	⇓	Most personal areas in this category have been resolved by the *HTMP*
Government Services	Low	⇓	Most personal areas in this category have been resolved by the *HTMP*
Utility & Infrastructure	Low	⇓	Most personal areas in this category have been resolved by the *HTMP*
Communications and Computer	Low to Medium	⇓	There may still be some residual problems, but most failures will have occurred and been resolved by the *HTMP*
Employment & Income security	Low to Medium	⇔	Residual employment and business related problems resulting from economic and supply-chain causal factors; eventually these decline toward mid to end of the *HTMP*
Banking & Finance	Medium	⇔	Fine tune allocation of financial assets, investments, retirement accounts, 401K, etc. Residual economic related problems resulting from supply-chain, litigation, and business failure causal factors; eventually these decline toward mid to end of the *HTMP*
Personal Assets	Low	⇓	Most personal areas in this category have been resolved by the *HTMP*

The risk factors listed in the preceding chart are reference values only. They indicate relative risk factor for this *millennium period* and do not necessary indicate whether a failure will occur and whether it will affect your family, your business, or you. It is important that you evaluate your own risk for this period and take appropriate action in terms of preparation and diversification in order to minimize risk exposure, even during this final *millennium period*. Review this chart frequently as this period approaches and add any new items that you download from the website *y2kbook.8m.com* or other locations.

Post-Transition Millennium Period
<u>Preparation Checklist</u>

❑ Stabilize any area of your portfolio that has suffered damage or failure
❑ Continue vigilance against fraud and scams
❑ Continue to monitor account statements and financial statements to ensure that no secondary or late Y2K related failures occur
❑ Slowly reallocate your portfolio toward growth type investments as the global economy pulls out of any recessionary period
❑ Reduce or eliminate any unnecessary bank or financial diversification accounts that were set up for the *CTMP*
❑ Look for signs of newly emerging companies and products that help the economy to recover
❑ Watch for signs of business failures and announcements of supply-chain failures that may drive Y2K related litigation

---

Identifying personal risks and developing a plan

Now that we have had a chance to thoroughly explore examples of the problems that might occur at the turn of the century, we have a good idea of what to look for. What we need to do now is to take a slow careful look around us and identify the products, goods, services that we depend upon and have come to take for granted. We then need to assess each of these items for risk and determine what the effect will be upon us if they were to suddenly not be available for an unknown period of time. We have built an understanding of supply-chain in the preceding chapters and must now apply this concept to our personal lives in order to customize a preparation plan that makes sense for our families, our businesses, and ourselves.

The list of categories that we need to look at should roughly parallel our "pyramid of needs" as defined by the famous writer and philosopher Thomas Maslow. Humans seem to need the basic necessities of life first like food, shelter, water, clothing, safety-items, etc. We next need things like companionship, ego, social stature and wealth, and then finally self-fulfillment.

With the Y2K problem, our basic needs such as shelter and clothing should be unaffected as long as we have these items to start with or are near them. If we are in some remote location, such as on vacation in a remote location or Caribbean Island and found ourselves stranded, then we might look at this item differently. What would be the chance that there might be a power grid problem at a hotel in Mexico or Central American Country, at the millennium? Although the larger cities of these countries are relatively stable in terms of technology, the risk is still probably greater than if you were in the US. Since there is no guarantee that all US locations are immune from problems, it is safe to assume that a foreign country may have a greater risk of failure, if for no other reason than not spending the time and resources Y2K testing that was spent in the US. Is this a risk that we are willing to take? Maybe, maybe not. It again depends upon our own affinity to risk and where we fit on the Millennium Risk Continuum chart discussed in chapter 2.

For the most part, this book has been focused on a pragmatic look at calculating risk for the millennium and should have helped the reader prepare for the unknown, if for no other reason than by raising awareness. The issue that needs to be addressed is that if you decide to book a trip to Mexico or some part of Europe during the millennium transition, you have already answered the question about your own tolerance to risk. One person I talked to told me that he wanted to go to New Zealand for the millennium because that was a location closest to the international timeline and would be changing to year 2000 before any other location in the world. That is fine, but you must build your preparation plan accordingly so that you are ready for whatever happens regardless of where you are, in case there are problems or failures that occur that affect your ability to return when you planned.

The fact is that we have become a very mobile society. Many of us find ourselves moving and traveling around quite frequently and with little notice. Not that this is good or bad, but in this circumstance, unnecessary travel or movement during the *Critical Transition Millennium Period* can, and probably will, pose some extra logistical problems that must be prepared for.

Let us look at the items that will affect us around our homes and businesses and then we can make extensions to the *millennium period* preparation checklists to cover situations that we might find ourselves in, if we are away from our familiar territory.

As has been pointed out, to predict exactly what will happen at the millennium transition is nearly impossible. You can look at the various viewpoints and form your own opinions. It is more than likely that the actual effects will be worse than many people expected but will not be nearly as bad as the doomsday believers have predicted. So in looking at the aspects that will affect us, we must take into account a list of items such as that contained in Appendix C of this book and assess your personal risk in each of the four *millennium time periods*. Again, the millennium impact categories that must be addressed are Personal Protection, Government Services, Utility & infrastructure, Communication and computers, Employment & Income security, Banking & Finance, and Personal Assets.

The preceding chapters have looked at each of the *millennium impact categories* as a general risk class matrixed into each of the *millennium periods*, but let us take a look at the more specific items that fall into each of these seven major impact categories. The reader will find that many of these categories have interrelated themes, but that will have to do because these categories are the least common denominator to a very complex problem. The purpose is to help you to create your own personal checklist for each millennium period using the lists in this book as a baseline

The first item is *personal protection* that also can include asset protection. Under this heading falls items such as safeguarding yourself and your family from harm, but also includes the safeguarding of your valuables and assets. If the actual millennium passage and its related problems lead to social panic and chaos, whether it is widespread or localized, there could be a struggle between the "have" and the "have-nots". If you are the person who has prepared and you come into contact with someone or a group who has not, you could befall a predicament that is over your head. My general advice to people is to be low-key. As you prepare for the various periods following the advice in this book, part of the preparation process may need to be some degree of privacy. What I mean by privacy is not to be silent about the fact that you believe that there are risks and that you want to be prepared, because the more people are prepared the less will be the severity of the Y2K impact itself. Rather, the actual details of how you prepared, what you have stored, and where you have stored your emergency preparations should be the part that is kept private.

If, for instance, you choose to store bottled water, gasoline, cash, food, and an electrical generator for a two-week reserve period, it will be best to store these in a private location at your residence. It may be best not to tell others, other than immediate family members and close friends, about its existence or location.

Another item that falls into this *personal safety* category is taking extra precautions during simple banking or shopping functions within a several week period of January 1, 2000. We have already discussed the possibility that people may begin to rush banks and ATM machines once they find out that the supply of available cash cannot meet the sudden demand. Remember that some of the country's largest banks and brokerage firms are already planning for security forces to be deployed around their locations and data centers in anticipation of the rush on money and assets in the time-period just before and right after the millennium passage. This event is not being taken lightly by the experts and neither should it be taken lightly by you! Because nobody can accurately predict the scope and the magnitude of the Y2K problem then it is probably safe to assume that extra precautions are a reasonable measure to take. The main issue is to prepare a plan of how to keep a low profile and to protect your personal assets from theft, looting, or harm by those who suddenly become desperate if a failure adversely affects them. I still don't believe that this will be a widespread problem, but I do believe that there is a remote chance that certain failures such as prolonged power outage or unavailability of cash and ATM machines could cause some behavioral panic in some locations. Your risk level will be different if you live in the country than if you live in the city. Remember the LA riots? It didn't take much to set them off and the possibility exists that something like this could happen again with the right set of triggering circumstances.

Another part of this safety category is the use of security systems. If these systems include silent alarms using phone lines to the police, you may need to rethink the security that you expect from such a system. If there is a power failure caused by an overload or brownout in the powergrid during the *Critical Transition Millennium Period*, there may be a disruption in telecommunication service leaving the property unprotected.

The timeframe I would worry most about, and thus focus your time planning for, is the time period immediately following the millennium passage. Most of the safety issues should be resolved within the first several days to a week. Any emergency rations of food, water, and fuel should sustain your family and you for a week to be safe. It is possible that isolated areas may be stricken for longer periods, but my general recommendation is to prepare for a week to two weeks of service disruptions. If the power grid and other utilities serving your area are stabilized sooner, then you can expect the inconveniences to end sooner, as well.

The next major *millennium impact category* is *government services*. President Clinton signed an executive order relating to the government's Y2K readiness in February 1998. This is in response to a number of reports and studies that were prepared by the Government Accounting Office (GAO) and consultants who were engaged by specific government agencies to assess and analyze the Y2K threat and estimate costs and time to achieve readiness. These reports suggested that the federal government was grossly unprepared for the millennium passage and rated a number of the agencies with grades like Ds and Cs in terms of overall preparedness. These reports also provided estimates that indicated that the government probably could not completely ensure a problem free transgression of the millennium passage and that efforts should be immediately taken to minimize problems in the most critical systems.

Was does this mean to the millions of people who depend upon Social Security, Medicare, Medicaid, and Welfare related systems to provide necessary subsistence for them? What does this mean to the Federal Aviation Administration (FAA) that guards our airports and skies by issuing aircraft takeoff and landing clearances for airlines based upon computer monitored airborne spacing? What does this mean to our nations defense and military that depend upon computers that might, or might not, be affected with the Y2K bug? The answer is that we don't know for sure, but President Clinton's executive order provided a sense of urgency to do everything possible to find and correct the errors in the most critical of the nations computer systems.

The problem is that the Presidential Order was signed far too late in order that the necessary testing of the billions of lines of computer code could be thoroughly tested in time for the millennium passage. The net effect is that some of us depend upon the government more than others, but all of us either directly depend or know somebody who depends on the government for their living and subsistence. Remember our discussion about "supply-chain"? This is certainly one place where we must look at the government and its level of adequate testing and preparation as a weak link in the supply-chain that affects almost everybody we know, in one way or another.

Unfortunately, there are many aspects of the government service impact category that we simply have no control over. We have simply depended upon our government to provide these services to us, or for us, and we have taken for granted that they will always work.

The fact is that this problem is not only limited to the federal government. There are other systems at the state and local government levels that are also a source of the risks that can affect us. It is currently up to the states themselves to test their systems and place the changes in the computers programs that control them. It is quite possible that these systems are more or less as unprepared as the Federal Government systems seem to be. One of the areas that remain in question is the interface between State and Federal systems. These interfaces are data gateways that have been built over time to share information and to facilitate cooperation between various governmental agencies. These interfaces are susceptible to Y2K data and system corruption and must be closely monitored by an agency that believes that its systems are otherwise Y2K sterile.

Most of the ways that a failure of certain government systems will affect us will be financial, record keeping, fiscal management, and taxation related. These areas are profound enough, but in order to realize the gravity of the situation, we need to look at a specific example where a single government agency related failure can quickly compound along the supply-chain into a drastic affect of the private and corporate sector.

There are areas such as we discussed with the FAA regarding air traffic that can have a profound affect on our commerce. If the FAA believes, and it does, that there is a potential problem with safety of flight of commercial aircraft during the *Critical Transition Millennium Period*. It could possibly force the cancellation of many airline flights so air traffic controllers can manually control aircraft separation in our nations airway system. This could be true until the FAA is comfortable with the ability of the air traffic control system radar's ability to meet its intended function safely. Considering that our nation's 20 largest airports alone account for literally thousands of flights per day, this one factor can have a huge effect on day to day business.

What if for a period of a month or more, half of those flights were cancelled? Would this not cause a chain reaction that could affect our nations, if not the world's commerce? Would not this cause an affect on those people who are employed by the airlines and related service companies? What about the corporations that makes up commercial America? What if salesmen could not reach their clients for a period of a month or more? Would this not affect the companies who employ them?

This specific example affects many people I work with directly because they travel many times a month to visit with and service clients in a sales and consultative role. This most certainly has to be factored into personal readiness plan by the traveling warriors for at least the first month of the new century. It is not that we should be afraid to fly due to safety concerns, but rather we should be concerned with the possibility of being stranded somewhere and not being able to get back to where we need to be during a crisis. Any long-term plans that you need to make for travel in this period should wait until February 2000. At least, at this point many of the issues can be worked out and air traffic related systems can be returned to a normal flow. I would definitely recommend the use of paper tickets rather than electronic tickets to make sure that you can work around system failures by the airlines that could lose your reservation and create other problems relating to bartering with other carriers. I would check a number of times with the airline to make sure that they still have the record of your purchase and reservation right until the day you leave for the airport. You might think that this precaution is unnecessary, but I believe that many people may be stranded or suffer unnecessary problems during the *Critical Transition Millennium Period*. The extra precaution is needed just to avoid periods of inconvenience, or worse.

Before you dismiss this concern for air travel as unnecessary, consider that early in 1998, the FAA reported to Congress that air traffic control systems reply upon aged mainframe computers which IBM has stated are not, and due to their age and architecture, cannot be made *Y2K ready*.

From another federal agency's perspective, consider that the Internal Revenue Service has between 60 and 100 million lines of computer programming code that is filled with reference to date periods. The agency computer administrator reported to congress during 1998 that it was questionable that they would complete system testing by the millennium passage. What does this mean to taxpayers and the federal treasury of the US for the fiscal year 2000? Is this a boon to the taxpayer or a liability to the country? These two are mutually exclusive.

Each of the different government agencies have taken their fiduciary duty to the American people seriously and have worked diligently to prepare their constituents for a continuity of service. The problem and the challenge for both the state and the federal government agencies has been the staffing and retention of qualified people who can test and fix the billions of lines of computer code before it is too late.

A responsible reader should assume to themselves that there is at least a remote risk that some of these systems could introduce millennium failures that can and probably will affect the people who depend upon those services for their living and subsistence. It is also reasonable then to assume that this failure will have a trickle affect into the economy to at least some percent of the population. That same responsible reader would then begin to believe that it is prudent to build a contingency plan for themselves or their loved ones to help bridge the time period until that service or subsistence can be restored. The government has announced that subsistence checks and electronic transfers such as Social Security will be issued during December 1999 instead of January. This is important because those who depend upon these payments for living will be covered for January. Will the government have its act together in time for the February payment?

The nature of your contingency plan should take the form of storing a several months reserve of that subsistence, be it money or foodstamps, to bridge the gap. The problem with the systems of today is that there has been a substantial move toward "electronic" rather than paper benefit payments from many of the governmental agencies in an effort to reduce the possibility of fraud and to reduce backoffice administration costs of mailing paper checks. These electronic benefits involve an electronic transfer of the entitlement directly into the recipient' bank accounts or into an online account that they debit using a special entitlement card. This has been very effective in cutting down on fraud and waste but has opened up the possibility of wholesale system breakdown with no manual capacity to replace the electronic funds, if the electronic system that provides for millions of transactions per week fails.

It will be up to the reader to make sure that they do not become a victim of a governmental system that they have no control over. Most reasonable people would believe that at least a month worth of reserve would be sufficient. I would encourage the readers to begin their investigation early in 1999 to find out from the government agencies that they depend upon what the status of their particular Y2K readiness and testing efforts are. An answer of work in process is not adequate.

The third major millennium risk impact category is *utility and infrastructure*. Included in this category is electric, water, sewer, gas, mass transit, traffic light control, street light control, and nuclear power plants that produce power for the power grid, etc. Many of these items have become staples in our society that we depend upon and seldom consider losing except in cases of natural disaster.

Consider that the complex circuitry that controls a nuclear powerplant may be 20-30 years old. It is highly likely that the monitoring and control panel circuits for these plants can contain thousands of chips and that any one could cause conditions in that plant that might cause the operators to shut it down. This is why that the Nuclear Regulatory Commission is requiring 100% Y2K readiness statements by July 1, 1999 from all nuclear powerplant operators or requiring a plant shut down.

If enough of these utility problems and errors were to occur, cities that depend upon these plants for power could be forced to go to other already stressed power sources for electricity. The power outages and brownouts might last for a moment and they might be last for days.

Consider that for most of North America north of the "Mason-Dixon" line, the millennium passage occurs in the middle of winter, during the shortest light period of the calendar year. A reasonable deduction for the reader might be to expect that there is a remote chance, at least, that there might be a power outage in some of the major cities in the country. If they live in one that is affected, they will be glad that they had a plan and prepared for this loss of service. Most importantly, it is important that they prepared ahead of time in order to avoid the rush at the last minute as the millennium passage approaches.

It would be my expectation that by October of 1999, the press will be as fully focused on the millennium period and its related predictions of problems and failures as they were with Monica Lewinsky during 1998. If you decide to go buy batteries, candles, generators, flashlights, and portable heaters when year 2000 mania" sweeps the media in December 1999, you are sure to encounter long lines, empty shelves and ultimately panic and chaos.

Another set of related areas that should be mentioned as vulnerable are water treatment and wastewater plants. First, they require power to operate. Second they have the same kinds of Programmable Logistic Controllers (PLC) and microchip driven devices that are involved in the production and flow metering of power.

Programmers have gotten clever in the past twenty years and have programmed in peak demand routines into the control programs that reference time and date to regulate flow and handle metering operation. For example, less water is needed in a city at 4:00am then at 4:00pm. There are peak demand periods in different seasons such as July and August versus January and February. If there is a hidden date routine embedded in a microchip or controlling program, then plant operation can, and will be, affected.

A reader may determine that it makes sense to store enough drinking water to last for 2 weeks. It is reasonable to assume that if there is a problem with these systems resulting from millennium passage, it is probable that the systems can be restored within that time. Some people may decide that it makes more sense to store more water. The problem will be that water takes up considerable space and being the middle of winter, room temperature storage space may be at a premium.

By the way, a rough estimate of water requirements might be one gallon of water per adult person per day. Does it make sense to start storing drinking water containers in September or October 1999? I believe that it is reasonable to make this assumption. I would not want to be in the long lines in December trying to buy bottled water. You have probably figured out that much so far just by reading this book! Plan ahead and store your rations ahead of the HMP.

What about mass transit? Busses and taxis will run as long as they can obtain fuel, to do so. You might question the immediate availability of commuter trains, although they have few time operated components. The track switching mechanisms and the light timing computers and sequencers might have some problems, but that, too, is questionable. I would believe that the biggest problem with mass transit will be with the power supply problem that could stop the trains altogether. This would be the larger risk rather than the risk of problems with actual Y2K failures with the mechanical aspects of the trains.

My recommendation for your plan during this period is to arrange to work from home during the early part of the *Critical Transition Millennium Period*, if that is possible. If these problems do not happen than you can continue to go to your job as you have been. At least you have considered the possibility and were adequately prepared.

I would be willing to bet that there will be at least enough scattered outages and problems to make the first few days after the Millennium passage a chaotic adventure that you might want to avoid. I would concentrate your plan on building the items in the checklist that you might have to go without for some period. Items such as electricity, and water should be the minimums on the list. Make whatever arrangements you believe are required to ensure that you are ready in case things get out of hand during the first several days to a week after millennium passage.

I have had people ask me about the status of schools and day-care centers. I have no direct information to respond to these questions, but I would recommend that people assume that if there are problems with power distribution and infrastructure that schools will be closed. I would assume that most daycare centers would continue to operate unless there was utter chaos in a particular location. You need to judge for yourself and consider a contingency plan. It is fortunate that the millennium passage is over the weekend so most people will have a day or two to consider the consequences in the world around them in the weekend press.

Another one of the millennium risk impact category that is believed to be vulnerable at the millennium passage is the area of *communications and computers*. Examples of these items include: Personal, midrange, and mainframe computers, telephones, cellular phones, digital phones, corporation and government office telephone PBXs and switchboards, phone company switch office locations, and the internet. Each of these items is operated and depends upon millions of programs and microchips that must be considered Y2K susceptible. Failures in the supply-chain for any of these components can cause failures for any of its constituent users.

Many computers have been updated with later model processors that are certified as year 2000 ready and the underlying operating systems have been updated to the latest OS version which should ensure that a simple infrastructure failure won't bring these machines down.

As discussed previously, the status of the billions of lines of computer code that control the programs that run on these machines remains in question, at this time. Also it is quite possible that the microchips themselves are built on computer logic which may contain the date code problem. It can be generally assumed that any chips manufactured after 1997 had the corrections built in, but only the manufacturer can certify that for sure. The programming code of the operating systems of the computers and the equipment follow roughly the same rule of thumb. For instance, IBM certified to one of my clients that their OS2 operating system for year 2000 readiness starting with their Merlin (version 4.5) that was being released during 1998. They further cautioned that just because you have the latest operating system does not guarantee that an older program running on that OS platform version that contains errors will not fail.

The same holds true for Microsoft. Their original version of Windows 95 was not certified as year 2000 ready. Only the subsequent B release of Windows 95 is certified, as is Windows 98, and Windows NT version 4.5, but typically the user still needed to download a patch to the operating system. Corporate America has done a reasonably good job of keeping their computers updated with the latest operating system technology, but home computer and some government installations still can be found running on pre-certified operating systems.

It only takes a few hours to go to the appropriate website and download the patches necessary to make sure that your computer's operating system is ready. You should check on the status of both your home and your business computers to determine that their operating systems will not cause you problems.

America has come to depend upon the computers that run our communications infrastructure. The reader can make a reasonable assumption that there could be some millennium failures in this impact category sector that may affect the very minute by minute communication that we have come to take for granted. Examples of communications that could be susceptible can range from phone system switches used to control our corporate switchboards to the major switch computers used by our phone companies to control the all telephone, pager, cellular, and internet communications traffic. Computers of a variety of sizes and vintage govern, manage, and route all of these types of communications. The later models (mid 1980s to early 1990's) are the ones that should cause us most concern. It is these models that started to incorporate the smarter functions as the designing engineers incorporated functions that were date and time dependent. What would happen to our society and our economy if we were suddenly unable to receive or send phone calls? Considering that the same corporation's computer network probably travels through the same phone switching system or an identical one for redundancy, it stands to reason that such a failure would be catastrophic for business and the economy, if extended over any length of time.

One issue that I have heard is that the phone companies will be urging people not to pick up their phones at midnight on January 1, 2000 just to see if they have a dial tone. Apparently, they are concerned that this action alone could overload the switch circuits. Imagine the problem if hundreds of millions of people tried to use the phone at the same moment.

Remember that companies precautions of shutting down the power to their plants and computer systems was being cited as the reason for predictions of brownouts and power-grid overloads. Now we have another similar situation that the millennium passage may cause an indirect failure in another one of society's utility infrastructures.

We must consider the effects on our communications systems during the *Critical Transition Millennium Period* to be a real possibility. We must assume that the major local phone companies and the long distance companies including MCI Worldcom, Sprint, and AT&T are doing everything they can now to identify, fix, and test their systems for possible failures. We must also assume and hope that outages will be spotted and temporary. The problem is that we just don't know where the problem will surface and how long it will be until it can be fixed. We must prepare our checklist to reflect the possibility of service disruptions in this area.

One of the areas that the experts have only begun to analyze is the area of computer viruses that will prey upon the millennium passage. Viruses are insidious, hidden programs that are passed from computer to computer with a usual purpose of data destruction or system incapacitation. It is now being reported that there may be computer viruses that are lurking on the internet waiting for an invitation onto host computers and networks attached silently to emails or downloaded programs to wreak additional havoc right after the millennium passage. As though we didn't have enough problems with the errors we are dreading that were created by accident, now we have to be weary of those that were invented on purpose. These programs are typically written by computer hackers and computer terrorists and have posed a significant threat and inconvenience to many that have come into contact with them in the past. For instance, there is a virus known as Michelangelo. The Michelangelo virus only affects computers that it is installed on when the computer system clock strikes March 6th, Michelangelo's birthday. It can render the target computer useless.

There are a number of companies that sell anti-virus software that can be installed on a computer to find and irradiate known viruses, which number into the thousands. It is highly advisable for readers to look into companies such as Norton Utilities and IBM Anti-virus and a number of other excellent programs that can be located at your local software store or by a quick search on the internet. It is important that you install or download the updates which come out nearly monthly to update new versions of viruses that are identified as the millennium date draws closer. This way any last minute discoveries of viruses will be automatically added to your anti-virus program running on your computer. Watch the Y2K related websites suc as *http://www.y2kbook.8m.com/* for news concerning computer viruses that may become problematic at the millennium passage.

Some people ask why you can't reset your computer system clock at the end of 1999 back to 1989, for instance, to avoid the whole millennium passage issue. In general, that may be a practical step for the home computer owner to ensure that no virus damage occurs to our system, but it is probably not a step that corporate and governmental computer users. In the next chapter, I will list detailed steps that you can take to test your personal electronic equipment, including computers. For now, the problem with resetting the system clock back to a previous date is that many computer files are sorted and indexed by creation date and by resetting the clock, the computer losses track of program and file versions and the ability to determine the latest version of them. Perhaps this is the lesser evil.

On a corporate basis, this is not practical because there are literally millions of computers that are cooperating on the corporate networks. The potential loss of audit trail of file versions and data date-stamping for proper recording of financial transactions, interest calculations, and many other items would wreak havoc on those organizations ability to conduct business. These organizations do not want to arbitrarily introduce problems into their computers and networks unless they have carefully calculated the benefits and results. Do not arbitrarily do change any setting on your work or business computer unless you are instructed to do so by your information systems department. They should release very specific instructions to employees about how to deal with Y2K related failures and failure prevention.

For many computers and programs, the millennium failure problem can be divided into two failure categories. The first is whether the program can handle the year 2000 by reconciling that the representation of the year '99' plus one is "00" after the millennium passage at midnight on December 31, 1999. The other, and perhaps more critical is whether it can handle the problem at the instant that the clock strikes midnight.

It is believed that there are many millennium related failure problems that can be averted or minimized by simply changing the system clock time to after midnight so the computer doesn't have to deal with the "stroke of midnight" problem. We will deal with this issue in the next chapter on testing electronics, but for now consider that there are settings that can be made to computers to minimize the risks for operating system and software failures.

The fifth major millennium impact category is *employment and income security*. This, like the others, is a broad category, but it quickly can summarize some of the major personal effects the millennium passage will have on of us.

We talked earlier about supply-chains and how the failure of a critical supplier to our employer could effect the very ability of our employer to stay in business. Look at the example of the airlines. If the FAA issues a mandatory cutback in flight slots while it monitors flight safety aspects of the air traffic control system during the millennium passage, what happens to all the airline employees? Chances are they will be idle for a period of time and there is a real chance that the airlines may layoff a large percentage of workers, if the delay is sustained.

What can we as workers do to protect ourselves? There may not be much we can do except ride out the storm, but we can at least be aware of our employment situation and know whether our employer is supply-chain susceptible. What we also can do is to prepare ourselves with a rainy-day cash reserve. The financial planning experts have been telling us for years that we should have 3–6 months cash reserve on hand. The fact is that we need to look at our employers and our positions with them carefully in the *Pre-Millennium Period* during our preparation and planning stage. As a general rule, smaller companies may be less likely to weather a disruption in supply-chain as a large company, but that may not be true for all.

Certain small companies may not relay upon any automated or susceptible suppliers and may in fact be the predominant supplier for a particular product or service. There will be a period of inventory build-up by many companies seeking to protect themselves for the approaching millennium period.

Another example of a small company that may be immune to supply-chain problems is a landscaping business. This business can continue to operate where a high precision machine tool company making parts for automobiles or aircraft may be devastated by an unexpected supply-chain failure concerning themselves or a work stoppage at the company they provide to.

To determine a strategy for protection across the *millennium period*, one must look at the risk their employer faces. An employer, big or small, that has a single supplier or a single customer is much more vulnerable than one that is diversified. This is true for all aspects of supply-chain analysis.

What can we as employees do to protect ourselves? You, as an employee of that company, can urge your superiors using this book as compelling evidence of the need to diversify its supply-chain. This can be in the form of providing for a wider host of customers and suppliers to reduce the risk of work stoppage during the millennium passage and the millennium periods that follow.

The problem is that many of us have little, if any, influence on the business of our employers and that we may be left to fend for ourselves. The fact is that in a complex society like ours, the economy is highly integrated and few people or businesses are able to escape the grips of this web of integration. That becomes the largest factor with the millennium and the associated Y2K related problem. We are simply woven too tightly with those in our personal and professional supply-chains and the chain reaction of failures that can, and probably will, occur during the *Critical Transition Millennium Period*.

The twelve months following will be more than many of us can afford to prepare for to avoid hardships. The best advice that can be drawn from this text is too prepare financially as best that you can and diversify your holdings to avoid loss or undue inconvenience from secondary failure in the banking or financial system in the *Critical* and *Post Transitional Millennium Periods*.

This brings us to the next major area of the major millennium impact categories; *banking and finance*. Banking and finance are going to be an extremely important area for many of us because failures in this supply-chain will wreak havoc upon the worlds economy quickly and completely. We saw with the global financial crisis of 1998 quickly sweep around the globe and affect us in our own country.

We observed the fact that not only can a physical failure or recessionary weakness of the banking system in a foreign country quickly affect us, but also the perceived weakness and the mood of investors can have just as real of an effect. This is very important to us as we prepare for the millennium passage because this event has both physical and emotional ramifications that can affect the economy and the financial markets quickly and completely.

So far in 1999, the US market continues to surge ahead and grow, despite the fact that the causes of the Asian financial crisis of 1998 have yet to be resolved. Further more, the Russian economy is in shambles and appears headed for further ruin and possible collapse, before it will get better. This brings the focus to the American economy. How many times can the Federal Reserve drop the interest rates distracting the market before the reality of the looming millennium threat and the continued threat of global recession takes over the US and the global economy? This is a real issue that we must address for ourselves.

We must determine just how much risk that we are willing to take, and how long we are going to take it before we take corrective, or better yet, preventative action. Issuing advice relating to pulling money from the financial markets is not only irresponsible, but also callously dangerous. Unfortunately, considering human nature, people will do it anyway and the results will be devastating.

The fact remains that other than our paycheck, which for most people pays for our immediate living needs, our personal wealth and standard of living fluctuates from day to day with the relative strengths of the stock, bond, and commodity markets. As we learned with the great depression of the 1920s and to a lessor extent during major market corrections in the 1970s, 1980s and 1990s, a single day can set back our net worth in increments of large percentages.

What we must do is to diversify our holdings in such a way that we can still enjoy the growth of the market, but also have portions of our portfolios that are in fixed rate and even protected asset pools such as equity funds and bank CDs. It would be advantageous with the approaching millennium period to diversify our holdings into a number of strong financial institutions that we have investigated and personally found to be sound in their Y2K related preparations and assurances. This might tend to make us question the hundreds of mutual funds that seem to emerge weekly as a safe place to harbor our money as millennium passage draws near.

In the discussion concerning the preparation of our personal plan during the various *millennium periods*, we spent quite some time exploring the topic of financial preparation prior to the *Hyper-Millennium Period* that will begin in late November 1999. Our plans for responsible asset reallocation and proactive diversification must be made prior to this period and the execution must begin well before this, as well. If we wait, we will not be able to escape the crushing blows to the economy and the financial markets that are sure to occur when the investors finally begin to deal with the inevitability and volatility of the millennium passage. As stated earlier, the millennium passage itself may only mark the beginning of a prolonged market downturn whose reverberations are sure to follow for months after.

In determining our personal strategy for fund and asset allocation, we must again look at our willingness to accept risk and build a plan around that risk tolerance. Any time we deal with the microeconomics of economic recession, there are certain types of financial instruments that stand out. Some people might move some of their investments to precious metals, some to bonds, some to CDs, some might decide that having cash is best. The advice that you can derive from this book is that each of these strategies has certain appropriateness for certain people with certain risk tolerances and they all have been based on a plan of some sort. I urge you to contact a certified financial planner to determine the best strategy for your personal financial situation. I urge you to do this as quickly as possible so that you can take advantage of relatively reasonable barriers to entry in some of these alternative financial instruments. The longer that you wait to seek the advice of an expert, the more difficult will be the resulting damage that you may sustain making the changes in your portfolio to prepare you for the subsequent transitional *millennium periods*.

The last major millennium impact category is Personal Assets. This category is a catch-all for all of the personal vehicles, computers, and electronic devices that we have and use that may be affected by the millennium passage and its affects on computer controlled circuits that reference time and date algorithms.

For the most part, it can be assumed with a high degree of accuracy that a device without a clock and one that has no calendar reference will not be affected. I have witnessed certain claims relating to the Y2K bug that billions of computer chips with hidden date reference will be shutting down at the millennium passage. The fact is that this is not a concern that we should be worrying about. A microchip or a software program coded into an electrical device should have no determination of any date, let alone the millennium passage date.

Take for instance an electronic coffee maker with a clock function. The clock has no idea of the date and therefore has no *Y2K susceptibility*. Think how many times such a device is plugged and unplugged and the clock is reset starting at 12:00am. The same holds true with many clock radios. They have time functions but do not have date functions. This is a very important distinction for all of us to make so we are not worrying about the irrelevant things taking our attention away from the important things. We must evaluate the devices that we have and we must quickly identify the devices that we own that are of risk.

In the chapter on testing personal devices, there will be a great deal of information about how to test a device such as a modern VCR or a Camcorder. I will show you step by step how to check it for Y2K susceptibility and how to determine what will happen to the device by manually setting it ahead to December 31, 1999 near midnight. With many devices such as a VCR, you may find that it does have a problem, yet will continue to function in a diminished capacity.

How can we use all of this information to prepare a specific Y2K readiness plan without becoming part of the Y2K problem? The fact is that we need to address our specific needs and adversity to risk and take these into account and build them into our readiness plan. If you are reading this information during the earlier part of 1999, then you have plenty of time to build a sound plan that will help you transgress into the next millennium with a minimum of disruption and inconvenience.

In order to build your plan, you can use the plan outline contained in Appendix C and the checklists included at the end of each millennium period chapter. These sections contain detailed checklists and relative risk assessments of the major millennium impact categories so you can determine which portions of the plan are most critical to your particular circumstances. In addition, you can visit the many websites such as *www.year2000.com* and *http://www.y2kbook.8m.com/* and receive a lot more valuable information about plan preparation. On these websites, there will be timely information posted and published that will help you keep up to date. There also will be monthly newsletters that will help you learn about the latest developments in Y2K related preparation by corporations, the government, and the world financial markets.

Testing electronic devices and software

One question that is asked quite frequently is about how to determine if personal electronic assets will still be operational after January 1, 2000. I believe that this topic deserves some discussion so that you have a chance to test your devices and determine for yourself the status of your belongings.

In general, most devices don't have a clock and calendar function that will be affected by Y2K. Many devices have clock functions such as coffee makers, clock radios, car dashboards, and VCR cameras, but will probably continue to operate and function fine after millennium passage. The main distinction of those devices vulnerable to the Y2K bug is whether their operation is built around the day of the week and day of the month and whether there are any special functions built into the operational software which controls the device that depend upon these functions.

One susceptible device that would apply to many US homes and businesses is the personal or business desktop computer and the various software titles that are installed on it. You would think that Microsoft would have identified and resolved the Y2K crisis for its operating systems long before it did, but that is not the case.

In order to ensure Y2K readiness for your particular PC operating system, you will probably need to download a software patch for that particular operating system. For instance, you can go to the Microsoft website, click on *software updates* or *software downloads* and then follow the hyperlinks to your particular operating system menu pages. I just recently helped a client download the Windows 98 Y2K software patch for their home business computer system. Windows 98 does a nice job of keeping up with software updates on your computer. Earlier versions of the Windows operating

103

system were not as "intelligent" at keeping track of updates. If you have Windows 95 or NT, you can get the respective patches on the Microsoft web site. If you have DOS, Win 3.1 or earlier Windows releases, you may be out of luck, as far as Y2K updates.

If you are fortunate enough to own an Apple Macintosh, then you are already "*Y2K ready*" because Apple released the Macintosh from the very beginning with a 4 digit date. That is not an absolute guarantee that other software that operates on the Macintosh is Y2K Ready, but at least the operating system is ok.

Just as with the Macintosh example just mentioned, you must be wary when it comes to all computers software in relation to their operating system. Just because the operating system is *Y2K ready* does not mean that the software installed on that computer is immune from having a Y2K related problem.

What kinds of software might encounter a problem, you might ask? Typically accounting, time management, calendar management, certain spreadsheet, and certain database management systems will be suspect because they typically have some time and date management and sorting routines built into them. Be aware that many software titles use license and installation management software algorithms that may not have anything to do with the function of the program. Many trial games and programs downloaded from the Internet use this method as a way to entice you to register them with the rightful owner.

Another example of personal devices that might have a problem is an electronic organizer. I have a model that has a calendar function built into it. I can specify what day and time of the week that I want an appointment and it must discriminate by using software built into its circuits which day of the week corresponds with what dates in the future and the past. A unit that is functioning correctly would know that January 1, 2000 is a Saturday and Tuesday, February 29, 2000 is a valid day of leap year.

Many late model VCRs have a similar function because they allow you to specify in advance that they are to record a show in the future on a particular day and time. A coffee maker has a time function, but is completely unaware of the date. The average car clock is also quite unaware of the date. Be careful though! The late 1980's GM Cadillac had a computer that would greet you with "Good Morning (or good evening), it is Wednesday, February17, 1999", for instance. This device was wonderful for its time period. The software built into it was very sophisticated and could easily determine leap year and would always know, if set correctly, that a leap year had 29 days in February. This is the type of hardware and software that should be suspect and ought to be tested in advance. Similar functions could be built into industrial trucks, farm tractors, and other equipment to prevent the operation beyond certain maintenance operation periods that have been preprogrammed into the devices control computers. Check with the manufacturer about whether your equipment has any of these functions built in that could pose a problem following millennium passage.

One issue that needs to be addressed is to determine what will happen to your equipment when the year is 2000 and to determine if there is any way that you can test the equipment ahead of time. There are several schools of thought on testing equipment like this. These devices, like computers and software all around the world, will either work correctly, display "1900" and cause other unpredictable results, or shut down all together. If the device continues to function normally except for displaying the incorrect date and time, then we say that the unit is "*Y2K susceptible*". If the unit goes blank, acts erroneously or unpredictably, or starts generating erroneous reports, answers, or displays, then we say that the device is "*Y2K damaged*". It is useful for us to know which of our devices will act in which way and it is also useful to know if there is a "work around" that will allow for continued operation of the unit even though it has suffered some type of Y2K related failure.

We can test these devices very easily and make our determination of how to properly complete our Y2K related preparations. One way is to simply go into the device or software controls and change the date and see what happens. Be aware that there are several distinct tests that must be accomplished in order to determine that your device (or software) is completely "*Y2K ready*".

In regards to Y2K testing, you should standardize on three main designations for Y2K as summarized in appendix E. A device or software is either "*Y2K ready*", "*Y2K susceptible*", or "*Y2K damaged*". "*Y2K ready*" means that the device or software has passed both millennium tests; transversal of time-date change to the year 2000, and transversal of year 2000 leap year. If any of these conditions are not met and the device cannot perform any function for which it has been designed as a result of a Y2K related failure, then it is "*Y2K susceptible*". *Y2K susceptible* devices can continue to function, but at some diminished capacity. "Y2K" damaged devices are devices that have been completely or largely incapacitated as a result of a Y2K related failure. Their primary functions are inaccessible, unresettable, or unbypassable to function beyond the year 1999. These are the ones that we want to know about, hopefully in a way that we don't incapacitatethem during the testing process! In some cases these devices or software can be corrected by the manufacturer and in others they can't. Either way, you will want to know as soon as possible, not when everyone else is calling customer service or clogging the company's web site trying to download software patches.

Let us try a number of tests on various devices so that you know exactly how to test your personal and business electronic assets and software. Important! Before you begin any test of this nature, you should backup your system and backup your software files so that you do not lose or affect any critical data. Chances are there will be no major issues with your device or software, but you must exercise caution!

The first test is to be sure that the device or software can transverse the calendar-change at the stroke of midnight. Enter the clock function of your device and set it for December 31, 1999. Now enter the clock setup function and set it for 12:59pm. Exit the setup function and simply watch and see what happens. Wait several minutes then try to access all of the functions of the device or software. Now enter the clock and calendar setup functions again. Is everything set correctly? Is the device keeping the proper time and displaying the proper date? If it is then you have completed this portion of the test successfully. If it isn't then you have determined that you have a "*Y2K susceptible*" device. Try resetting the system clock and calendar back to the current date and restart the device. Is it working correctly now? If it is then now try to reset the clock and the calendar ahead to Saturday, January 1, 2000 with a time of anything past midnight. Now exit the setup function and see if the device is operating correctly.

It is possible that a device or software can operate with the clock and calendar set beyond the midnight millennium passage time, but not function at the actual stroke of midnight. Some companies I have talked to have adopted this strategy toward their Y2K readiness posture. They plan to shut down their data centers and computer systems just before midnight and restart them after midnight to avoid the actual problems associated with the actual moment of millennium passage. If this is the situation with your device or software, then note this and try the other two tests to determine the total capacity with which the software or device will operate beyond 1999.

The second test is to evaluate the device or software's performance with leap year in the year 2000. Enter the clock function of your device or software and set it for Monday, February 28, 2000. Now enter the clock setup function and set it for 12:59pm. Exit the setup function and simply watch and see what happens. Wait several minutes then try to access all of the functions of the device or software. Now enter the clock and calendar setup functions again. Is everything set correctly? Is the device keeping the proper time and displaying the proper date of Tuesday, February 29, 2000? If it is then you have completed this portion of the test successfully. If it isn't then you have determined that you have a "*Y2K susceptible*" device. Try resetting the system clock and calendar back to the current date and restart the device. Is it working correctly now? If it is then now try to reset the clock and the calendar ahead to Tuesday, February 29, 2000 with a time of anything past midnight. Now exit the setup function and see if the device is operating correctly. If it is then, you should note that this device needs special attention at leap year.

If the device or software shows the wrong date or time as a result of either of these tests, then check the device or the software to determine if all other functions are working properly. If they are, then there is probably no harm done, but you have determined that you have a device or software that is "*Y2K susceptible*". If the device starts acting peculiarly or is locked up in any way, then you have a device or software that is "*Y2K damaged*". If you can't get the device or software to operate to get the clock and calendar function back to 1999, then you have encountered a "Y2K hard failure". This is the worst kind and is the least likely to be encountered, but is not impossible to occur. If this is the case then try removing the power from the device or rebooting your computer, whichever the case may be.

In the case of software that behaves like this, uninstall the software from the computer and reinstall it with the current 1999 time and date set in the operating system clock. This should allow the software or device to begin routine operation again for the time being, but be aware that this software or device will not be functional beyond the millennium passage time.

How did your personal devices do? Did you have any problems? Most of the devices and software that we own will not have any problem at all. Unfortunately, it is not these types of software and devices that will cause the problems at the actual millennium passage. It will be the major computers and the computer networks of the government and the corporations all over the world that will cause the major disruptions that will affect us in the end.

Now, hopefully you have a better appreciation for the testing that governments, corporations, and organizations are going through and the steps needed to protect themselves and to protect their customers from the insidious failures related to the Y2K.

Conclusion

My sincere hope is that you have had a chance to read this book in time to put the necessary plans in place that will ensure a minimal impact of the millennium passage and its fallout on your family, your business, and you. By far, the most important time to put the actions and plans in place is during the *Pre-Millennium Period*. This is the time when you can make logical choices and wise purchases of reserve supplies. It is also the best time to proactively diversify and reallocate your financial assets and financial investments without encountering long lines of people and significant delays. It is far better to be placing orders for new accounts and financial portfolio reallocations and diversification before the madness of failure or economic hardship sets in.

If you do nothing else as a result of reading this book but have an increased awareness, then hopefully you will still feel that it was worthwhile. There is no guarantee that anything will happen other than receiving a few bills that have the balance listed incorrectly. I don't personally believe that this will be the full extent of the Y2K related problems and, hopefully by now, neither should you.

Making changes to the way that we conduct our lives is not an easy thing to do, especially during a period of remarkable economic growth and viability as is being experienced now in the US.

Many of us simply do not have the resources or the control over our lives to make such changes. We humans are reactionary creatures by design. Others of us simply don't have the time or the energy to worry about it. Others of us may simply hope that someone else will take care of the problems or figure that we can address the problems when they occur. Honestly, if you have made it this far through this book and still feel that way, then I will be really surprised.

If I can summarize the points made throughout this book, I would do it as follows: Investigate your risks using the outlines in the appendix of this book and review the risk assessment checklists included in the millennium period chapters.

Determine and investigate your supply-chain and learn who provides you with critical supplies, products, and services. Learn what their weaknesses are and determine if there are ways to work around their weaknesses.

Investigate the components of your personal supply-chain and identify the weak links in the chain. Start early to plan and prepare for the millennium passage. Don't by lulled into waiting until it is too late.

Diversify your holdings and your assets so your financial risk is minimized and the risk of harm is reduced to a minimum.

Don't depend on any single business or institution to be available because you may be disappointed.

Take care of your financial obligations for January 2000 in December, if possible. Prepay any credit accounts that you have or consolidate them so that you have a minimum exposure to billing errors and related concerns.

Don't wait until the last minute to stock up on supplies and cash. Build your reserve supply gradually and keep its location and existence private.

Avoid risky situations during the first several hours to several days of the year 2000 until you know that your safety is not in jeopardy.

Make copies and organize your accounts and statements and lock in a secure location; you may need these to help reconcile with companies after unexpected Y2K related failures occur.

Expect service disruptions for at least the first several days to a week of the *CTMP* immediately following January 1, 2000. If they don't occur in your location, then you can consider yourself lucky.

Do not listen to the people who tell you not to worry and be wary of people who try to get you to worry to much for their own benefit.

If you follow these suggestions then you will probably make it through the millennium passage with a minimum of harm. Be aware that there may be secondary problems or business failures that may take months to materialize or be made public. Watch for any warning signs during the first six months of the year 2000. Even strong companies may come under pressure as litigation is filed by people and organizations who feel that they were harmed by delays in service or perceived lack of preparation on the parts of the strong companies. This repercussion could have an affect on your portfolio and investments for months and up to a year after the actual millennium passage itself.

Preparation will be the key to your success. It will not happen without your persistent attention to details as the millennium event approaches and eventually passes. There will be enough of those around and that is not a group that you want to share membership with. Preserve the American Dream at all costs, and by all means, avoid being a victim of Y2K!

Appendix A:
Millennium Time Periods

Pre-Millennium Period (*PMP*)
Entire 1998 through November 30 1999
Period of discovery, denial, rumors, confusion, positioning by both corporations and government entities

Hyper-Millennium Period (HMP)
December 1, 1999 through 11:59pm, December 31, 1999
Period of hype, panic, panic buying near end of period, US markets now falling as the fear of Y2K related effects are contemplated, investors begin pulling funds from the market further deepening recession. Households run on cash reserves driving short-term interest rates up.

Critical Transition Millennium Period (CTMP)
12:01am January 1, 2000 through March 31, 2000
Period of computer induced mechanical failure, computer report and database induced errors and failures, recession deepens as the complete effects of Y2K related failure around the world finally surface

Post-Transition Millennium Period (PTMP)
April 1, 2000 through June 1, 2001
Period of computer induced reporting, taxation related computer report and database induced errors and failures will continue while recession begins to ease, eventually events revert to normal after final tax periods, annual reports, etc. finally run correctly. Financial markets begin to recover.

Appendix B:
Major Millennium Impact Categories

1. Personal Safety

2. Government Services

3. Utility & Infrastructure

4. Communications and Computer

5. Employment & Income security

6. Banking & Finance

7. Personal Assets

Appendix C:
Millennium Period Risk Summary Chart

Risk Category	Relative Risk Factor: Pre-Millennium Period	Relative Risk Factor: Hyper-Millennium Period	Relative Risk Factor: Critical Transition Millennium Period	Relative Risk Factor: Post-Transition Millennium Period
Personal Prep & Safety				
Safety	None	Low	High	Low
Shelter	None	None	Medium	Low
Medical	None	None	Medium	None
Food	None	Low	Medium	Low
Water	None	Low	Medium	Low
Fuel Reserved	None	None	Medium	Low
Personal Transportation	None	None	Low	Low
Cash Reserved	None	High	High	Low
Asset Protection	None	Low	High	Low
Travel Plans	None	Low	High	Low
General Inconvenience	None	Medium	High	Medium
Medicine Storage	None	None	Medium	Low
Warmth	None	None	Medium	Low
Elevators	None	None	High	Low
Proximity from home at Y2K	None	None	High	Low
Other				
Other				

Government Services				
Public Transportation	None	None	Medium	Low
Communication and News	None	None	Low	Low
Information	None	None	Low	Low
Air Traffic Control	None	None	High	Low
Police Protection	None	Low	Medium	Low
Public Aid & Social Security	None	Low	Medium	Low
Mail Delivery service	None	Low	Low	Low
Emergency Services	None	Low	Medium	Low
Other				
Other				
Utility & Infrastructure				
Water	None	Low	Medium	Low
Power	None	Low	High	Low
Sanitation	None	Low	Low	Low
Heat/ Cooling	None	Low	Medium	Low
Natural Gas	None	Low	Medium	Low
Other				
Other				
Employment & Income security				
Income Protection	None	Low	High	Low
Paycheck delivery method	None	Low	Medium	Low
Electronic deposit	None	Low	Medium	Low
Scams or fraud	Low	Medium	High	Low
IRA, Pension, fund withdrawals	None	High	High	Low
Other				
Other				

Communications and Computer				
Risk of Billing/Accounting Errors	Low	Medium	High	Medium
Personal Computer OS	Low	Low	Low	Low
Personal Computer Software	Low	Low	Medium	Low
Telephone/fax/internet	Low	Low	Low	Low
Cellular Phone & Service	Low	Low	Low	Low
Long Distance Carrier	Low	Low	Low	Low
Internet access	Low	Low	Low	Low
Other				
Banking & Finance				
Investment Allocation	Low	High	High	Low
Important Documents Protection	Low	Medium	High	Low
Insurance Policies	Low	Medium	Medium	Low
Retirement plans	Low	Medium	Medium	Low
Stocks and bonds	Low	Medium	High	Low
Copies of all statements	Low	Medium	High	Low
Backup Bank accounts	Low	Medium	High	Low
Credit card accounts	Low	Low	High	Low
Debit card accounts	Low	Low	High	Low
Brokerage accounts	Low	Low	High	Low
ATM and cash access	Low	High	High	Low
Taxes and tax accounts	Low	Low	Medium	Low
Other				

Personal Assets				
Personal Electronics	Low	Low	Medium	Low
Personal Entertainment	Low	Low	Low	Low
Automobile electronics	Low	Low	Low	Low
Household devices	None	Low	Low	Low
Other				
Other				

Appendix D:

Device and Software Y2K test result categories

Test Applied and Result	Y2K Ready	Y2K *susceptible*	Y2K Damaged
Time & Calendar December 31, 1999 Transition Test			
Operates normally	Go to Leap year Test		
Operates, but with diminished capacity		X	
One or more major functions fail to operate, or locks up			X
Time & Calendar February 29, 2000 Leap Year Test			
Operates normally	X		
Operates, but with diminished capacity		X	
One or more major functions fail to operate, or locks up			X

Biography

Michael G. Gaffney

Author of

"Y2K and the American Dream"

Michael Gaffney has been consulting, authoring, teaching, and presenting to business and high technology audiences for 15 years. Using a dynamic and spirited presentation and narrative style, his practical approach to this important topic provides insightful and timely information about the topic of Y2K readiness, both from personal and professional fronts. Mr. Gaffney, an MBA whose specialty has been finance and macroeconomics, is currently the Manager of Application Solutions for Compuware Corporation, a company known for its leadership in software technology including Year 2000 readiness. He guides a team of "Enterprise Solution" consultants who implement integrated client server and web-based computer systems to solve critical business challenges using Compuware Corporation's UNIFACE software development language and related integration products.

In the 1970's, he was certified as a commercial pilot, FAA Certified Flight and Ground Instructor, and a FAA Certified Aircraft Mechanic. In the 1980's, he was awarded an MBA and was an outspoken pioneer in the use of Artificial Intelligence and Expert Systems to aid corporations in leveraging the knowledge of their business experts to help business run more efficiently. In the 1990's, he has been an outspoken advocate for "Open" multi-tiered computer systems and Object-based technology to promote widespread software reuse as a driver for competitive advantage in business. He has presented to countless clients, technical and business oriented conferences, meetings, and organizations throughout the last fifteen years. He has taught classes and seminars in Aviation Meteorology, Instrument Pilot Ground School, System's Analysis, Design, Programming, Object Oriented Programming, and Technology Utilization for

 *Managers. His "ROI Expert" software program was featured in PC Week magazine in 1987 and has been sold in 12 countries since. He is highly acclaimed by those who have benefited from his speeches, classes, presentations, articles, and white papers.*

WWW.Y2KBOOK.8M.COM